Janice VanCleave's

Earth Science for Every Kid

Other Wiley books by Janice Pratt VanCleave:

Biology for Every Kid: 101 Easy Experiments that Really Work

Chemistry for Every Kid: 101 Easy Experiments that Really Work

Also forthcoming:

Janice VanCleave's Astronomy for Every Kid: 101 Easy Experiments that Really Work

Janice VanCleave's Physics for Every Kid: 101 Easy Experiments in Motion, Heat, Light, Machines, and Sound

Janice VanCleave's
Earth Science for Every Kid
101 Easy Experiments that Really Work

Janice Pratt VanCleave

John Wiley & Sons, Inc.
New York • Chichester • Brisbane • Toronto • Singapore

Illustrated by Barbara Clark

In recognition of the importance of preserving what has been written, it is a policy of John Wiley & Sons, Inc., to have books of enduring value published in the United States printed on acid-free paper, and we exert our best efforts to that end.

Library of Congress Cataloging-in-Publication Data

VanCleave, Janice Pratt.
    Janice VanCleave's earth science for every kid : 101 experiments that really work / Janice Pratt VanCleave.
      p.   cm. — (Wiley science editions)
    Summary: Instructions for experiments, each introducing a different earth science concept.
    ISBN 0-471-53010-7 (pbk.).—ISBN 0-471-54389-6 (lib. bdg.)
    1. Earth sciences—Experiments—Juvenile literature. [1. Earth sciences—Experiments. 2. Experiments.] I. Title.
QE29.V36   1991
550'.78—dc20   90-42724

Printed in the United States of America

91 92 10 9 8 7 6 5 4 3 2 1

Dedicated to my father,
Raymond Eugene Pratt

Preface

This is an elementary science experiment book, and like its predecessors *Chemistry for Every Kid* and *Biology for Every Kid,* it is designed to teach that *Science is fun!* Earth science is more than a list of facts about rocks, atmosphere, oceans, earthquakes, and flowing rivers. It is a study of how your life is affected by the things on and around the earth. The 101 earth science experiments are designed for children ages 8 through 12. Young children will be able to successfully complete the experiments with adult supervision. Older children can easily follow the step-by-step instructions and complete the experiments with little or no adult help. Special warnings are given when adult assistance might be required.

The book contains 101 experiments relating to earth science. Each experiment has a purpose, a list of materials, step-by-step instructions, illustrations, expected results, and a scientific explanation in understandable terms.

The introductory purpose for each experiment gives the reader a clue to the concept that will be introduced. The purpose is complete enough to present the goal but does not give away the mystery of the results.

Materials are needed, but in all the experiments the necessary items are easily obtained. Most of the materials are readily available around the house. A list of the necessary supplies is given for each experiment.

Detailed step-by-step instructions are given along with illustrations. Pretesting of all the activities preceded the drafting of the instructions. The experiments are *safe* and they *work*.

Expected results are described to direct the experimenter further. They provide immediate positive reinforcement to the student who has performed the experiment properly, and they help correct the student who doesn't achieve the desired results.

Another special feature of the book is the Why? section, which gives a scientific explanation for each result in terms easily understood.

This book was written to provide safe, workable earth science experiments. The objective of the book is to make the learning of what happens on and around our habitat—the earth—a rewarding experience and thus stimulate your desire to seek more knowledge about science.

Note:

The experiments and activities in this book should be performed with care and according to the instructions provided. Any person conducting a scientific experiment should read the instructions before beginning the experiment. An adult should supervise young readers who undertake the experiments and activities featured in this book. The publisher accepts no responsibility for any damage caused or sustained while performing the experiments or activities covered by this book.

Acknowledgments

I wish to express by appreciation to special friends who have helped by pretesting the activities or just giving moral support when I needed it: David, Cindy, and Daniel Nolen; Ruth Ethridge; Jacque Toland; Sandra Kilpatrick; David and Holly Ruiz; Nancy Rothband; Jo Childs; and Ron Ross.

Sue Plaunt, a first grade teacher at San Antonio Academy, San Antonio, Texas, agreed to have her students pretest experiments used in this book. I am thankful to these young scientists for their help: Michael Andersen, Thomas Berg, Reeves Craig, Patrick Farrow, Matthew Gainey, Joey Gamez, Ryan Gaston, Jaques Gauna, Casey Guthrie, Jonathan Lankford, Andrew Morrill, Oscar Ordaz, Eric Pesina, Jesse Rosada, Reagan Sadovsky, Mark Santos, Ram Srinivasan, William Stanley, Scott Sunde, Matthew Talley, Frank Tejeda, Paul Thomas, Joseph Vives, Matthew Wagner, Toby Wayman, James Wood, and Jeromy Wuneburger.

A special note of gratitude to the members of my family who volunteer their time and sometimes unknowingly do some of the pretesting. These very special helpers are: Russell, Ginger, Kimberly, Jennifer, David, Tina, and Davin VanCleave; as well as Calvin, Ginger, and Lauren Russell; Raymond, Rachel, Ryan, Dennis, Brenda, Carol, Erin, and

Amber Pratt; Patsy and Kenneth Henderson; Kenneth, Dianne, Kenneth Roy, and Robert Fleming; and Craig, Kymie, Krystie, Allen, and Megan Witcher.

My husband, Wade, receives my deepest gratitude. His love and encouragement are invaluable.

May I never forget that God is the author of science, and how much fun He has provided in allowing me to discover a small part of His wonderful creation.

Janice VanCleave

x

Contents

Introduction

Earth science is the study of the unique habitat that all known living creatures share—the earth. This science includes information from other sciences. Physics, chemistry, biology, astronomy as well as geology experiments are included to give you a better understanding of the earth and its place in space. Studying earth science, like studying all sciences, is a way of solving problems and discovering why things happen the way they do. It seems that we have always tried to explain the world around us. Early myths describe gods that race across the sky in sun chariots or throw thunderbolts to the earth. These myths explained events that were observed but not understood. As time passed, each generation gathered new information, and slowly, knowledge about the earth has been accumulated. The wonderful fact that there is still so very much to learn and understand should excite all young scientists and encourage them to seek answers to unsolved problems and question things presented as fact. Scientists identify a problem and seek solutions through research and experimentation. Science began and continues due to our own curiosity. This book may not lead to any new scientific discoveries, but it will provide fun experiments that teach known earth science concepts.

This book will help you to make the most of the exciting scientific era in which we live. It will guide you in discovering answers to questions relating to earth science such as: Why is the sky blue? Why does the earth wobble? What causes a volcanic eruption? What happens during an earthquake? What causes dew to form? How can a diamond be cut so smoothly. What is inside the earth? How does rock movement produce heat? Where does rain come from and where does it go? The answers to these questions and many more will be discovered by performing the fun, safe, and workable experiments in this book.

You will be rewarded with successful experiments if you read an experiment carefully, follow each step in order, and do not substitute equipment. It is suggested that the experiments within a group be performed in order. There is some build-up of information from the first to the last, but any terms defined in a previous experiment can be found in the glossary. A goal of this book is to guide you through the steps necessary in successfully completing a science experiment and to teach you the best method of solving problems and discovering answers. The following list gives the standard pattern for each experiment in the book:

1. Purpose: This states the basic goals for the experiment.
2. Materials: A list of necessary supplies.
3. Procedure: Step-by-step instructions on how to perform the experiment.
4. Results: An explanation stating exactly what is expected to happen. This is an immediate learning tool. If the expected results are achieved, the experimenter has an immediate positive reinforcement. An error is also quickly

recognized, and the need to start over or make corrections is readily apparent.

5. Why?: An explanation of why the results were achieved is described in understandable terms. This means understandable to the reader who may not be familiar with scientific terms.

General Instructions for the Reader

1. **Read first.** Read each experiment completely before starting.
2. **Collect needed supplies.** You will experience less frustration and more fun if all the necessary materials for the experiments are ready for instant use. You lose your train of thought when you have to stop and search for supplies.
3. **Experiment.** Follow each step very carefully, never skip steps, and do not add your own. Safety is of the utmost importance, and by reading any experiment before starting, then following the instructions exactly, you can feel confident that no unexpected results will occur.
4. **Observe.** If your results are not the same as described in the experiment, carefully reread the instructions, and start over from the first step.

Measurement Substitutions

Measuring quantities described in this book are intended to be those commonly used in every kitchen. When specific amounts are given, you need to use a measuring instrument closest to the described amount. The quantities listed are not critical and a variation of very small amounts more or less will not alter the results.

The exchange between SI (metric) and English measurements will not be exact. A liter bottle can be substituted for a quart container even though there is a slight difference in their amounts. The list on page 5 is a substitution list and not an equivalent exchange.

English to SI Substitutions

English	SI (Metric)

LIQUID MEASUREMENTS

1 gallon	4 liters
1 quart	1 liter
1 pint	500 milliliters
1 cup (8 ounce)	250 milliliters
1 ounce	30 milliliters
1 tablespoon	15 milliliters
1 teaspoon	5 milliliters

LENGTH MEASUREMENTS

1 yard	1 meter
1 foot (12 inches)	1/3 meter
1 inch	2.54 centimeters
1 mile	1.61 kilometers

PRESSURE

14.7 pounds per square inch (PSI)	1 atmosphere

Abbreviations

atmosphere = atm
centimeter = cm
cup = c
gallon = gal.
pint = pt.
quart = qt.
ounce = oz.
tablespoon = T.
teaspoon = tsp.

liter = l
milliliter = ml
meter = m
millimeters = mm
kilometers = km
yard = yd.
foot = ft.
inch = in.

I

Earth in Space

1. Bulging Ball

Purpose To determine why the earth bulges at the equator.

Materials *construction paper — 16 in. (40 cm) long*
scissors
paper hole punch
ruler
paper glue
pencil

Procedure

- *Cut 2 separate strips, 1 1/4 in. × 16 in. (3 cm × 40 cm), from construction paper.*
- *Cross the strips at their centers and glue.*
- *Bring the four ends together, overlap, and glue, forming a sphere.*
- *Allow the glue to dry.*
- *Cut a hole through the center of the overlapped ends with the hole punch.*
- *Push about 2 in. (5 cm) of the pencil through the hole.*
- *Hold the pencil between your palms.*
- *Move your hands back and forth to make the paper sphere spin.*

Results While the sphere is spinning, the top and bottom of the strips flatten slightly, and the center bulges.

Why? The spinning sphere has a force that tends to move the paper strips outward, causing the top and bottom to flatten. The earth, like all rotating spheres, bulges at the

8

center and has some flattening at the poles. The difference between the distance around the earth at the equator and the distance around the earth at the poles is 44 miles (27.5 km).

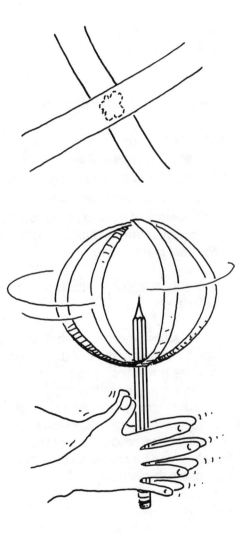

2. Precession

Purpose To demonstrate the movement of the earth's axis.

Materials *modeling clay*
round toothpick

Procedure

■ *Shape a piece of clay into a ball about the size of a marble.*

■ *Push the toothpick through the center of the clay ball so that just the tip of the pick sticks out one side.*

■ *Place the tip of the toothpick on a table.*

■ *Twirl the long end of the pick with your fingers.*

■ *Observe the movement of the top of the toothpick. Note: The ball spins poorly if the toothpick is not through the center or if the clay is not round.*

Results As the clay ball spins, the top of the toothpick moves in a circular path.

Why? As the ball spins, there is a shifting of the weight because the ball is not perfectly round. The earth, like the clay ball, wobbles as it rotates because of the slight bulge at the equator. The earth's axis (the imaginary line through the poles of the earth) moves in a circular path as the earth wobbles. This movement is called *precession.* The top of the toothpick makes many revolutions as the clay ball spins, but it takes 26,000 years for the earth to wobble enough for its axis to make one complete turn.

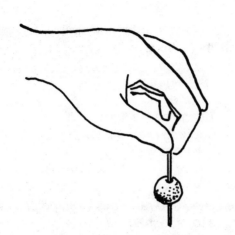

3. Wobbler

Purpose To demonstrate how the composition of the earth affects its motion.

Materials *marking pen*
1 raw egg
1 hard-boiled egg
Caution: *Have an adult hard boil the egg.*

Procedure

- *Allow the boiled and raw eggs to stand at room temperature for about 20 minutes.*
- *Mark numbers on each egg: boiled #1, raw #2.*
- *Place both eggs on a table, and try to spin each egg on its side.*

Results The hard-boiled egg spins easily and continues to spin for a few seconds. The raw egg wobbles and stops more quickly than the cooked egg.

Why? The material inside each shell affects the way it spins. The cooked egg has a solid content that spins with the shell. The liquid inside the raw egg does not start spinning with the movement of its shell. The outer shell motion does cause the liquid to move, but slowly. The sluggish movement of the liquid causes the egg to wobble and stop more quickly. Parts of the earth's mantle and outer core are liquid. The earth's interior is not solid, and like the egg, the earth wobbles during its rotations. Unlike the egg's wobbling, the earth's wobbling is very slight and takes many years for a noticeable change.

12

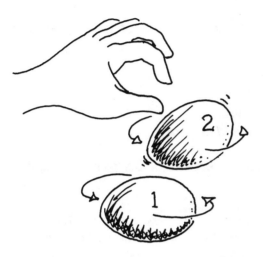

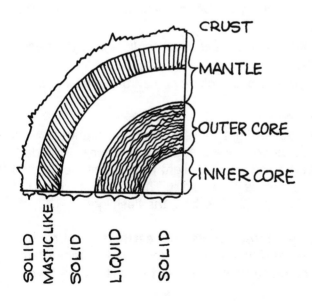

CRUST

MANTLE

OUTER CORE

INNER CORE

SOLID
MASTIC LIKE
SOLID
LIQUID
SOLID

4. Day and Night

Purpose To determine the cause of the day and night cycle.

Materials *table*
flashlight
dark shirt
small hand mirror

Note: This experiment needs to be performed at night.

Procedure
- *Place the flashlight on a table and turn it on. The flashlight is to be the only light source in the room.*
- *Stand about 12 in. (30 cm) from the flashlight wearing a dark shirt.*
- *Slowly turn toward your left until you face away from the flashlight.*
- *Hold the mirror at an angle to reflect light onto the back of your shirt.*
- *Complete your turn and observe the front of your shirt as you turn.*

Results A spot of light moves across your shirt toward your right side as you face the flashlight. Your shirt is dark when you turn away from the light until the reflected light from the mirror shines on the shirt. The reflected light is not as bright as the light directly from the flashlight.

Why? Your shirt represents the earth, the mirror the moon, and the flashlight the sun. Your turning imitates the rotation of the earth on its axis. As the earth turns toward the east, the light from the sun moves across the rotating earth. Daytime is experienced by the people on the side facing the sun, and reflected light from the moon brightens the side of the earth turned away from the sun. The night-time is very dark when the moon is not in position to reflect the sun's light onto the earth.

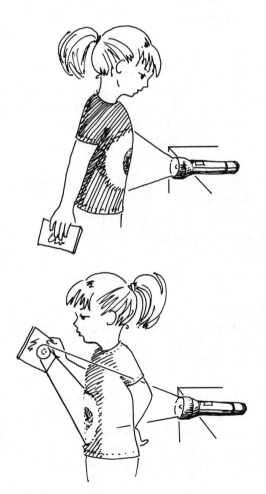

5. Tilt

Purpose To demonstrate the effect of the earth's tilt on seasons.

Materials *ball of modeling clay the size of an apple*
2 pencils
flashlight

Procedure

- *Insert a pencil through the ball of clay.*
- *Use the second pencil to mark the equator line around the center of the clay ball. This line should be halfway between the top and bottom of the ball.*
- *Position the ball on a table so that the pencil eraser is leaning slightly to the right.*
- *In a darkened room, place the flashlight about 6 in. (15 cm) from the left side of the ball.*
- *Observe where the light strikes the ball.*
- *Place the light about 6 in. (15 cm) from the right side of the clay ball.*
- *Observe where the light strikes the ball.*

Results The area below the equator receives the most light when the pencil eraser points away from the light, and the area above the equator is brighter when the pencil eraser points toward the light.

Why? The pencil represents the imaginary axis running through the earth. The Northern Hemisphere, the area above the equator, is warmed the most when the earth's axis points toward the sun. This is because more direct light rays hit the area. The Southern Hemisphere, the area below

16

the equator, receives the warming direct light rays when the earth's axis points away from the sun. The direction of the earth's axis changes very slightly during the earth's movement around the sun, causing the Southern and Northern Hemispheres to receive different amounts of light rays. This results in a change of seasons.

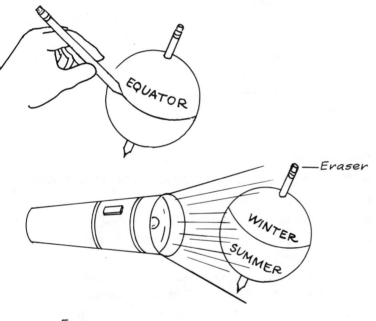

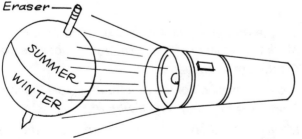

6. Mega-Weight

Purpose To demonstrate the difference in the masses of the atmosphere, hydrosphere, and lithosphere.

Materials *1 large paper clip*
paper cup, 10 oz. (300 ml)
string
ruler
scissors
cardboard, 3 1/4 in. × 12 in. (8 cm × 30 cm)
pencil
2 rubber bands
dirt
black felt-tip marker

Procedure

■ *Attach a paper clip to the top of the cardboard piece.*
■ *Tie two rubber bands together.*
■ *Hang the rubber bands on the paper clip.*
■ *Use a pencil to punch 2 holes under the rim of the cup on opposite sides.*
■ *Run the string through the end of the rubber band and tie the ends through each hole in the cup.*
■ *Hold the cardboard vertically so that the cup hangs freely.*
■ *Let the bottom of the top rubber band be the pointer. Mark the position of the pointer and label the mark Air.*
■ *Fill the cup with water.*
■ *Mark the position of the pointer and label the mark Water.*
■ *Empty the cup and refill it with dirt.*
■ *Mark the position of the pointer and label the mark Land.*

18

Results Comparing the weight of equal quantities of air, water, and dirt indicates that air is the lightest and dirt the heaviest material.

Why? The dirt used in the experiment does not contain all of the elements found in the *lithosphere.* The lithosphere is the part of the earth not including the air above the earth (the atmosphere) or the water on the earth (the hydro-sphere). This experiment indicates that dirt is heavier than air or water. A real sample of the lithosphere would have indicated that the lithosphere makes up about 99.97% of the total weight of the earth, with air contributing only .00009% of the weight and water about .024%.

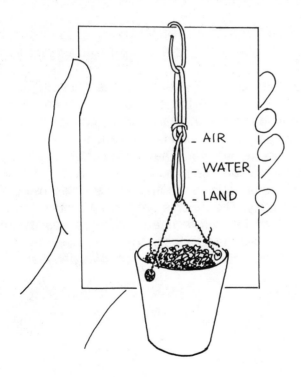

AIR

WATER

LAND

19

7. Eclipse

Purpose To demonstrate a solar eclipse.

Materials *tennis ball*
marble

Procedure
- *Place the tennis ball in your left hand.*
- *Hold the ball at arm's length in front of your face.*
- *With your right hand hold the marble in front of the ball.*
- *Close your left eye and slowly move the marble toward your open, right eye.*

Results As the marble nears your face, less and less of the ball is visible until finally the ball is no longer seen.

Why? The marble is smaller than is the ball, just as the moon is smaller than the sun, but they both are able to block out light when they are close to the observer. When the moon passes between the sun and the earth, it, like the marble, blocks out light. The blocking of the sun's light by the moon is called a *solar eclipse.* The moon moves around the earth about once a month, but a solar eclipse does not occur monthly. The moon's orbit is not around the earth's equator, and its axis is tilted, which causes the moon's shadow to miss the surface of the earth most of the time. A solar eclipse occurs three or fewer times per year.

II

Rocks and Minerals

8. Salty

Purpose To determine how salt beds are formed.

Materials *glass bowl, 2 qt. (2 liter)*
measuring cup, 1 cup (250 ml)
measuring spoon, tablespoon (15 ml)
table salt

Procedure

■ *Stir together in the bowl 1 cup (250 ml) of water and 4 tablespoons (60 ml) of salt.*

■ *Allow the bowl to sit undisturbed until all of the water evaporates. This may take 3 to 4 weeks.*

Results Cubic crystals line the bottom of the bowl, with white frosty deposits on the inner sides of the bowl.

Why? Beds of salt are believed to have formed from shallow ponds that were close enough to the ocean to collect salt water and were then cut off from the sea. Slow evaporation of the water in the pond, as in the bowl, left behind clear cubic salt crystals called halite. Climbing clumps of frosty salt are formed where water rises up the sides of the pond or container, and salt in the solution crystallizes as the water quickly evaporates. This fast drying does not allow the salt molecules to move into position to form cubic crystals. The random depositing of the salt molecules produces the frosty crystals.

DAVIN'S SALT

25

9. Needles

Purpose To demonstrate how crystals form.

Materials *measuring cup, 1 cup (250 ml)*
Epsom salts
measuring spoon, tablespoon (15 ml)
scissors
black construction paper
lid from a large jar

Procedure

■ *Cut a circle from the black paper that will fit inside the lid. Place the paper in the lid.*

■ *Fill the measuring cup with water (250 ml).*

■ *Add 4 tablespoons (60 ml) of Epsom salts to the water and stir.*

■ *Pour a very thin layer of the mixture into the lid.*

■ *Allow the lid to stand undisturbed for one day.*

Results Long needle-shaped crystals form on the black paper.

Why? The Epsom salts molecules move closer together as the water slowly evaporates from the solution. The salt molecules begin to line up in an orderly pattern and form long needle-shaped crystals. The salt molecules stack together like building blocks, and the shape of the molecules determines the resulting shape of the crystal.

10. Deposits

Purpose To demonstrate the formation of caliche deposits.

Materials *pickling lime (found with food canning supplies)*
1 large-mouthed jar, 1 qt. (1 liter)
measuring spoon, teaspoon (5 ml)
masking tape
marking pen

Procedure

- *Fill the jar half full with water.*
- *Add ¹/₂ teaspoon (2.5 ml) of lime to the water and stir.*
- *Place a piece of tape down the side of the jar.*
- *Mark the height of the liquid in the jar with the marking pen.*
- *Set the jar so that it will remain undisturbed.*
- *Observe the jar daily for 2 weeks.*

Results The water level drops, and a white crusty deposit forms above the water line on the inside of the jar.

Why? Like the jar of limewater, ground water contains large amounts of minerals, including calcium. When carbon dioxide gas from the air dissolves in the mineral water, a white solid called calcium carbonate is formed. As the water evaporates, a crust of white calcium carbonate is left. Large deposits of calcium carbonate are found in the semi-arid southwestern United States. These deposits, known as *caliche,* are found on or near the surface of the ground.

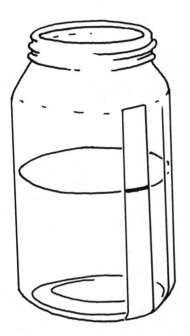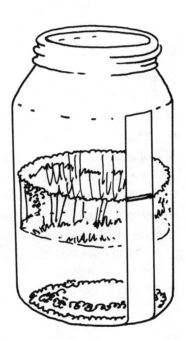

11. Dripper

Purpose To demonstrate the formation of stalagmites and stalactites.

Materials *Epsom salts*
2 small jars, such as baby food jars
cotton string
scissors
2 washers
spoon
ruler
paper

Procedure

- *Fill each jar with Epsom salts.*
- *Add water to the height of the Epsom salts.*
- *Stir.*
- *Cut a piece of string, 24 in. (60 cm).*
- *Tie a washer to each end of the string.*
- *Place one washer in each of the jars.*
- *Place a piece of paper between the jars.*
- *Position the jars so that the string hangs between them with the lowest part of the loop about 1 in. (2.5 cm) above the paper.*
- *Allow the jars to stand undisturbed and out of any draft for one week.*

Results Part of the epsom salt does not dissolve in the water, and the washers rest on top of the undissolved crystals. Water drips from the center of the loop onto the paper. A hard, white crust forms on the string and grows downward as time passes. A mound of white crystals builds up on the paper beneath the string.

Why? Water containing the Epsom salts moves through the string. As the water evaporates, crystals of Epsom salts are deposited. The Epsom salts formations are just models of how crystal deposits form in caves. Actually, calcium found in ground water mixes with carbonic acid (rain water plus carbon dioxide from the air), which seeps through the roof of the caves. As the water falls, small particles of calcium carbonate cling to the ceiling, eventually forming long spikes called stalactites. The water that reaches the floor evaporates, leaving the calcium carbonate deposits, which build to form stalagmites. The formation of these rocklike icicles is a very slow process; it takes many thousands of years for them to form.

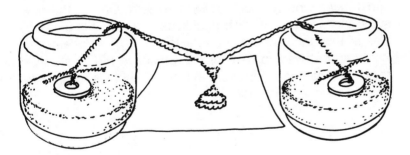

12. Bubbles

Purpose To demonstrate a positive test for limestone.

Materials   3 seashells
                vinegar
                glass

Procedure
- *Fill a glass one-quarter full with vinegar.*
- *Add the seashells.*

Results Bubbles start rising from the seashells.

Why? Vinegar is an acid and seashells are made of limestone, a mineral. Limestone chemically changes into new substances when in contact with an acid. One of the new substances formed is carbon dioxide gas, and it is the bubbles of this gas that are seen rising in the glass of vinegar. Acid can be used to test for the presence of limestone in rocks. If limestone is present in a rock, bubbles form when an acid touches the rock.

13. Spoon Pen

Purpose To demonstrate a mineral streak test.

Materials *unglazed porcelain tile (The back of any porcelain tile will work.)*
metal spoon (stainless steel)

Procedure
- *Rub the handle of the spoon across the back of the porcelain tile.*
- *Write your name on the back of the tile with the spoon handle.*

Results The spoon makes a dark grey mark on the white tile.

Why? A streak test is made by rubbing a mineral sample across a piece of unglazed porcelain. The color of the streak made is the same as the color of the powdered mineral. Grinding the spoon into a powder would produce the same dark grey color as is seen on the porcelain streak plate. The color of the streak made by a mineral can be an important clue in identifying the mineral.

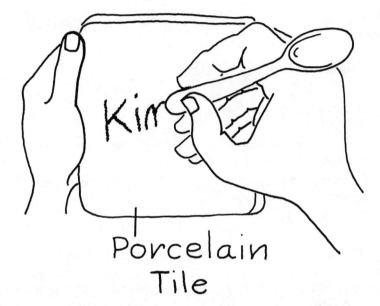

Porcelain
Tile

14. Crunch

Purpose To demonstrate the formation of metamorphic rocks.

Materials *20 flat toothpicks*
  book

Procedure
- *Snap the toothpicks in half, but leave them connected.*
- *Pile the toothpicks on a table.*
- *Place the book on top of the toothpick pile and press down.*
- *Remove the book.*

Results The toothpicks are pressed into flat layers.

Why? The toothpicks flatten into layers under the pressure of the book. In nature, the weight of rocks at the surface pushes down on rock and dirt beneath, forcing them to flatten into layers. Rocks formed by great pressure are called *metamorphic rock.*

15. Sedimentary Sandwich

Purpose To demonstrate a sedimentary rock formation.

Materials *2 slices of bread*
crunchy peanut butter
jelly
knife, for spreading
plate

Procedure

Note: Do this before lunch.

- *Lay one slice of bread on a plate.*
- *Use the knife to spread a layer of peanut butter on the slice of bread.*
- *Add a layer of jelly on top of the peanut butter layer.*
- *Place the second slice of bread on top of the jelly layer.*
- *Eat the sandwich.*
  Caution: Never taste anything in a laboratory setting unless you are sure that there are no harmful chemicals or materials. This experiment is safe.

Results A sandwich with a series of layers has been constructed.

Why? Sedimentary rocks are formed from loose particles that have been carried from one place to another and redeposited. These rocks usually are deposited in a series of layers similar to the layers in the sandwich. Each layer can be distinguished by differences in color, texture, and composition. The oldest layer and lowest bed is deposited first and the youngest layer is at the top. The layers over a period of time become compacted and cemented together to form solid rock structures.

16. Line-Up

Purpose To demonstrate that some minerals have a definite cleavage line.

Materials *paper towels*

Procedure
- *Try to rip a single sheet of a paper towel from top to bottom.*
- *Turn another sheet of paper towel and try to tear it from side to side.*

Results The paper will tear easily in one direction but not in the other.

Why? Paper towels are made on a wire screen, creating a straight line in one direction. Pulling on the paper attacks the weakest point. The parallel lines on the paper made by the wire screen are thinner than the rest of the paper, and thus the paper rips easily down one of these lines. Jagged and irregular tears result when the paper is pulled in the opposite direction. This is like cutting minerals, such as diamonds, along cleavage lines. The mineral splits smoothly and easily *along* the lines where the molecules line up, but it can smash into irregular pieces if hit *across* the cleavage line.

40

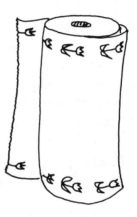

17. Sampler

Purpose To demonstrate core sampling.

Materials *3 different colors of modeling clay*
drinking straw
fingernail scissors

Procedure

- *Soften an egg-sized piece of each color of clay by squeezing it in your hands.*
- *Flatten the clay pieces, and stack them on top of each other to form a block about 1 in. (2.5 cm) deep.*
- *Push the straw through the layers of clay.*
- *Pull the tube out of the clay.*
- *Use the scissors to cut open the straw.*
- *Remove the clay plug.*

Results The straw cuts a cylinder-shaped sample from the layered stack of clay.

Why? As the straw cuts through the clay, the clay is pushed up inside the hollow tube. The captured clay is called a core sample, and it reveals what materials are layered inside the block of clay. Coring devices made of metal are used to cut through layers of soil just as the layers of clay were cut. The metal core sampler has a plunger that pushes the soil out so that it can be studied.

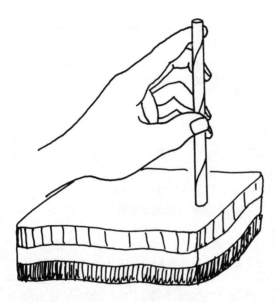

43

18. Sinkers

Purpose To demonstrate how placer ore deposits form.

Materials *glass jar with lid, 1 qt. (1 liter)*
5 paper clips
1 cup (250 ml) soil

Procedure
- *Fill the jar half full with water.*
- *Add the soil and paper clips.*
- *Close the lid and shake the jar vigorously.*
- *Allow the jar to stand undisturbed for 5 minutes.*

Results The paper clips fall quickly to the bottom of the jar, and the slower-moving soil settles on top of the clips.

Why? Most of the soil falls more slowly than the heavier paper clips, and thus a layer of soil forms on top of the paper clips. In nature, rain beats on top of the soil, shaking and softening it. The heavier materials in this wet mixture sink lower and lower as the years pass. Heavy grains of metal continue to sink until they reach a hard rock layer. Particles of metal that combine in this method are called *placer ore* deposits. These deposits are rich in metals.

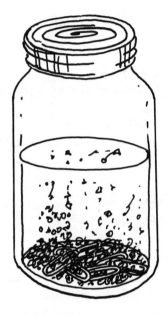

19. Wash Away

Purpose To demonstrate hydraulic mining.

Materials *empty coffee can*
10 paper clips
small pebbles —enough to line the bottom of the can
1 cup (250 ml) of soil
garden hose with spray nozzle

Procedure

Note: This is an outdoor activity.
- *Place the paper clips, pebbles, and soil in the can.*
- *Mix thoroughly.*
- *Place the can outside on the ground.*
- *Set the water nozzle on the high pressure position.*
- *Direct the stream of water into the can.*
- *Continue to spray the water into the can until the overflow water looks clean.*

Results The dirt is washed out of the can, leaving the pebbles and paper clips in the bottom of the can.

Why? Some of the soil dissolves in the water and some of it is light enough to be lifted and carried out of the can by the moving water. The paper clips and pebbles are too hard to be broken apart by the spraying water like the dirt particles. The heavier materials are not lifted by the water, so they remain in the bottom of the can. Rocks that contain metal are called *ores.* Ore deposits, especially placer deposits as described in Experiment 18, are mined with water.

Powerful streams of water are used to wash away the soil surrounding the ore. The rock pieces left are taken to refining plants where pure metals are removed. The process of mining with water is called *hydraulic mining*.

20. Prints

Purpose To determine how fossils were preserved.

Materials *paper plate*
paper cup
modeling clay
seashell
petroleum jelly
plaster of Paris
plastic spoon

Procedure

- *Place a piece of clay about the size of a lemon on the paper plate.*
- *Rub the outside of the seashell with petroleum jelly.*
- *Press the seashell into clay.*
- *Carefully remove the seashell so that a clear imprint of the shell remains in the clay.*
- *Mix 4 spoons of plaster of Paris with 2 spoons of water in the paper cup.*
- *Pour the plaster mixture into the imprint in the clay. Throw the paper cup and spoon away.*
- *Allow the plaster to harden, about 15 to 20 minutes.*
- *Separate the clay from the plaster mold.*

Results The clay has an imprint of the outside of the shell, and the plaster looks like the outside of the shell.

Why? The layer of clay and the plaster are both examples of fossils. The clay represents the soft mud of ancient times. Organisms made imprints in the mud. If nothing collected in the prints, the mud dried, forming what is now called a cast fossil. When sediments filled the imprint, a sedimentary rock formed with the print of the organism on the outside. This type of fossil is called a mold fossil.

21. Gulp!

Purpose To determine how fossils became embedded in ice.

Materials *refrigerator*
cake pan
rock about the size of your fist

Procedure

- *Fill the cake pan with water and place the pan in the freezer overnight to allow the water to freeze.*
- *Leave the pan of ice in the freezer and place the rock on top of the ice.*
- *Gently lift the rock every 10 minutes for one hour.*

Results At first, the rock can be lifted, but it sinks into the ice and the ice sticks to the rock holding it in place. This makes it difficult to lift.

Why? The heat of the rock causes the ice to melt, and the rock sinks. After the rock cools, it continues to very slowly sink in the ice. The weight of the rock pushes down on the ice, causing it to melt. The liquid water is cold enough to refreeze around the rock. The refreezing of this water is called *regelation*. Fossils are found deeply embedded in ice mainly because falling snow covered the organism, but also because the weight of the animal caused it to sink through the ice as did the rock on the pan of ice. The pressure of the organism melted the ice beneath it, and the cold water refroze as the animal sank deeper into the ice.

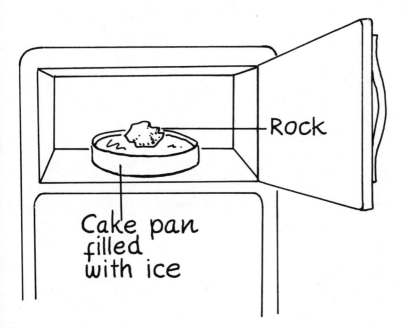

Rock

Cake pan filled with ice

III

Crustal Movement

22. Rub-A-Dub

Purpose To demonstrate the effect of heat produced by crustal movement.

Materials cardboard
glass soft-drink bottle
scissors
refrigerator
cup of water

Procedure

- Cut a circle from the cardboard that is slightly larger than the top of the bottle.
- Place the empty bottle in the freezer for 20 minutes.
- Remove the bottle from the freezer.
- Dip the cardboard into the cup of water and place the wet paper over the mouth of the bottle.
- Quickly rub the palms of your hands together about 20 times.
- Immediately place your hands around the outside of the bottle.

Results One side of the cardboard circle rises and falls.

Why? The moving and colliding of molecules emits heat energy. Rubbing your hands together produces heat, and this heat causes the cold air in the bottle to warm up and expand. This expanded gas pushes up on the paper with enough force to partially lift the paper and allow the hot gas to escape.

When sections of the earth's crust rub against each other as they move, the heat produced causes the rock material

54

to vibrate. If molecules in the solid rock move fast enough, they break away from each other, and the solid melts into magma (liquid rock beneath the ground). Further heating can cause the liquid to change into a gas. Most materials become larger when heated. Crustal changes such as earthquakes and volcanos occur when materials inside the earth expand, forcing heat, energy, and gaseous materials out through the earth's surface.

23. Shifting

Purpose To demonstrate continental separation.

Materials *cookie sheet*
dirt, 2 cups (0.5 liter)
bowl, 1 qt. (1 liter)
spoon

Procedure
- *Pour the dirt into the bowl.*
- *Add water and stir with a spoon until you have a thick mud.*
- *Pour the mud into the cookie sheet.*
- *Set the pan of mud in the sun for 2 to 3 days.*
- *Push down around the sides of the dried mud.*

Results The surface of the dried mud cake cracks.

Why? The mud is broken into pieces with jagged edges, and all the pieces fit together. The continents of the earth, like the mud cake, look like large jigsaw-puzzle pieces. The coastlines of the continents have irregular shapes that appear to fit together. In the past, pressures within the earth may have broken a large land mass into the pieces that now form the separate continents on the earth.

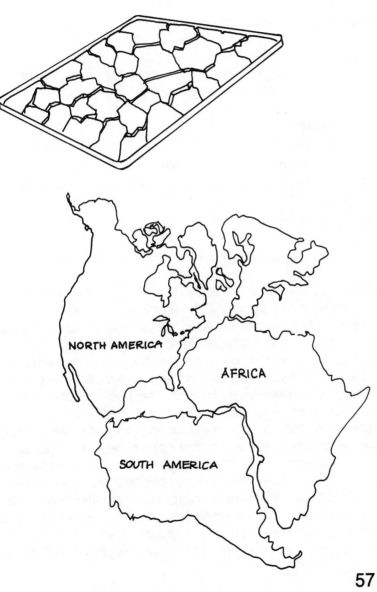

NORTH AMERICA

AFRICA

SOUTH AMERICA

57

24. Pop Top

Purpose To demonstrate how a geyser works.

Materials *funnel*
large coffee can or pot as tall as the funnel
plastic tubing about 1 yd. (1 m) long

Procedure

■ *Fill the pot with water.*

■ *Set the funnel mouth down into the water.*

■ *Place the end of the plastic tubing under the rim of the funnel.*

■ *Blow into the tubing.*

Results Water sprays out the funnel's tube.

Why? Blowing air under the funnel forces air bubbles up the stem of the funnel. As the air moves upward, it pushes water out the top of the tube. Geysers are funnel-shaped cracks in the earth that are filled by underground streams. When water in the lower part of the crack is heated to boiling, the bubbles of steam rise to the surface. A geyser erupts when water trapped in the neck of the funnel-shaped crack is forced out the top by the rising bubbles of steam. As long as you continue to blow under the funnel, water erupts out the top, but natural geysers erupt only when enough pressure builds up to force the water up and out the top of the crack. Some geysers erupt once every few minutes, while others erupt only once every few years. Old Faithful in Yellowstone National Park is an example of a geyser that erupts so regularily that a schedule of its display can be listed. This geyser erupts about every

70 minutes and has not missed an eruption in more than 80 years of observations. Geysers are rare; most of the world's geysers are in Iceland, New Zealand, and Yellowstone National Park.

25. Spreader

Purpose To demonstrate the expansion of the Atlantic Ocean.

Materials *scissors*
shoe box
modeling clay
sheet of paper

Procedure

- *Cut two 3 in. × 11 in. (7 cm × 28 cm) strips from a sheet of paper.*
- *Cut out a 0.5 in. × 3.5 in. (1 cm × 9 cm) section from the center of the bottom of the shoe box.*
- *Cut out a section in the center of one of the box's largest sides.*
- *Put the paper strips together, and run them up through the slit in the box.*
- *Pull the strips out about 3.5 in. (8 cm), and fold them back on opposite sides.*
- *Press a flattened strip of modeling clay about the size of a pencil on the end of each strip.*
- *Hold the papers under the box between your index and second finger.*
- *Slowly push the strips up though the slit.*

Results The clay pieces move away from each other as more paper moves upward.

Why? The clay represents continents bordering the Atlantic Ocean. The rising paper acts like the hot, molten rock moving out of the crack in the mid-ocean ridge. When liquid rock pushes through the ocean floor's surface, it forms a new layer on both sides of the crack. It is believed that this new material pushes against the old floor, causing it to spread. The Atlantic Ocean may be widening by about 1 in. (2.5 cm) each year. As the ocean widens, the continents of Europe and North America are moving apart as did the clay pieces.

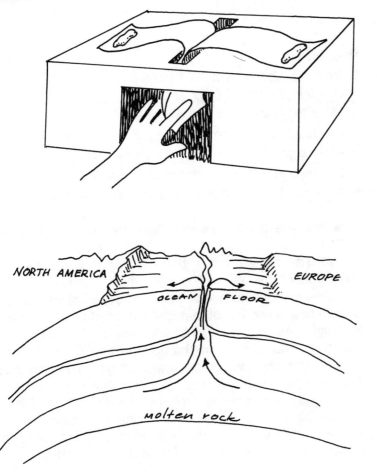

26. Dipper

Purpose To determine how ocean trenches (deep ocean valleys) are formed.

Materials *modeling clay—2 different colors*
small plastic soft-drink bottle
2 books

Procedure

- *Mold the clay to form a 2-layer rectangle about 1 in. × 3 in. × 6 in. (3 cm × 8 cm × 15 cm).*
- *Place the books 4 in. (10 cm) apart.*
- *Use the clay block to span the gap between the books.*
- *Add weight to the bottle by filling it with water.*
- *Set the bottle in the center of the clay block.*
- *Allow the bottle to remain undisturbed over night.*

Results The clay block bends downward under the bottle.

Why? The molten rock within the mantle of the earth is constantly on the move. The hot, lighter mantle rock rises, and the cooler, heavy rock sinks. The clay block demonstrates how a section of material can bend downward due to weight. As described in Experiment 25, hot liquid rock from the mantle pushes up through the cracks in the ocean, forming the underwater mountain range called the Mid-Atlantic ridge. The thin crust beneath the ocean is most affected by the movement of the mantle rock, and large valleys called trenches are formed where the mantle sinks. The spreading of the Atlantic Ocean may contribute to the forming of trenches. As the Atlantic Ocean is getting larger,

62

the Pacific Ocean is getting smaller. The heavy sections of the ocean floor are moving downward and sliding under the lighter land masses that border the Pacific Ocean, forming deep valleys and trenches along the edge of the land.

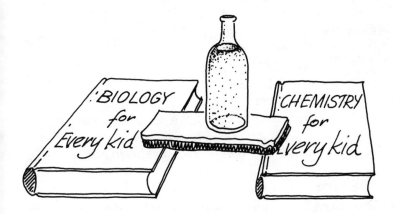

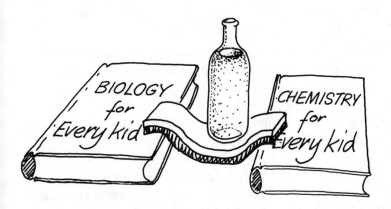

27. Dynamo

Purpose To demonstrate how a magnetic force field gives clues to the earth's internal structure.

Materials *large iron nail (20d, commonly called a 20-penny nail)*
wire (#18 gauge)
6-volt battery
small cardboard box
iron filings (like those found in toys such as Magnetic Disguise®)
Note: *Iron filings are available in hobby shops.*

Procedure

■ *Use the nail to make a hole in the center of the box and another hole on one of the sides of the box.*
■ *Wrap the wire around the nail, from top to bottom, leaving at least 6 in. (15 cm) of wire at both ends.*
■ *Insert the wire-wrapped nail in the hole.*
■ *Attach one end of the wire to each of two battery poles.*
■ *Sprinkle iron filings on top of the box around the nail.*
■ *Tap the box gently to spread the iron filings.*

Results The iron filings spread out in a starburst pattern around the wire-wrapped nail.

Why? The iron filings are pulled toward the wire, forming the starburst pattern, because moving electrons produce a magnetic field, and as the electrons flow through the wire, a magnetic field forms around the wire. The magnetic field around the earth may be the result of moving electrons. An explanation for electron movement is that the earth has an inner molten metal core. As the earth turns, electrons are knocked free from the rotating liquid metal. The production of the earth's magnetic field by the rotation of the earth is called the *dynamo theory.*

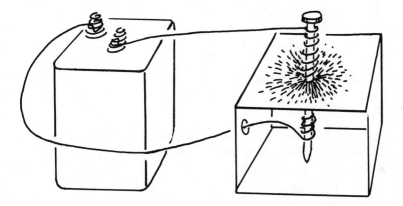

28. Swingers

Purpose To determine if the north end of a magnet always points to the earth's magnetic North Pole.

Materials *compass*
sewing thread
2 steel straight pins
cellophane tape
scissors
paper
ruler
magnet

Procedure

■ *Place the heads of the pins on the ends of the magnet so that their points face each other.*

■ *Cut two rectangles about 1/2 in. × 1/4 in. (2 cm × 1 cm) from the paper.*

■ *Cut a 12 in. (30 cm) and a 24 in. (60 cm) piece of thread.*

■ *Attach one thread to each of the rectangular pieces of paper.*

■ *Insert one pin in each of the pieces of paper.*

■ *Tape the ends of the threads to the top of a door opening, about 12 in. (30 cm) apart.*

■ *Observe the direction in which the heads of the pins point.*

■ *Use a compass to determine the direction the pins are pointing.*

Results The head of one pin points south and other points north.

66

Why? The earth behaves as if a large bar magnet is inside it causing magnetic materials to be attracted to its opposite ends. The north end of this imaginary magnet produces the earth's north magnetic pole, and the north ends of all magnets are attracted to this pole. The north ends of magnets are really north-seeking poles. You are temporarily lining up the electrons in the pins when you put them in contact with a magnet. Placing the pins on the magnet in opposite directions causes the head of one pin and the point of the other pin to be north-seeking poles.

29. Stretch

Purpose To demonstrate the effect of a tension force.

Materials *balloon*
marking pen

Procedure
- *Draw a square on a deflated balloon.*
- *Divide the square into three sections.*
- *Use the marking pen to color the two outer sections on the square.*
- *Inflate the balloon and observe the markings.*
- *Deflate the balloon and again observe the markings.*

Results The drawing spreads out in all directions when the balloon is inflated. If the balloon has not been inflated too much, it will recover its original shape and size when deflated.

Why? The rubber molecules in the balloon are being pulled apart by the pressure of the air inside. Parts of the balloon stretch more than others, causing a change in the shape of the diagram drawn on the rubber. Tension is a stretching or pulling-apart force. If the force is not too great, solids in the crust with elastic properties like the balloon will recover their original shape and size when the force is removed. If the force is too strong, the rocks cannot remain together, and they break apart—as the balloon would if you continued to inflate it with air.

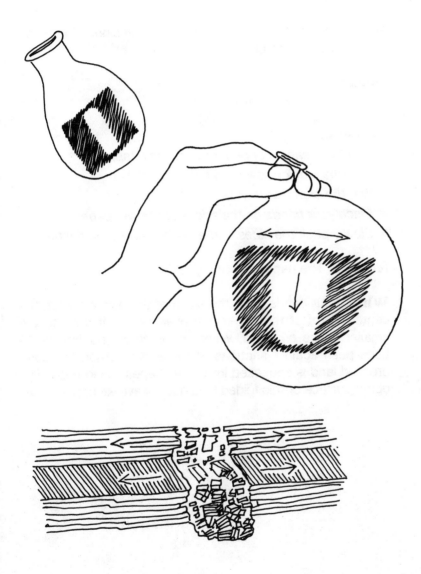

30. Folds

Purpose To demonstrate how compressional forces affect crustal movement.

Materials *4 sheets of paper towels*
glass of water

Procedure
- *Stack the sheets of paper towels on a table.*
- *Fold the stack of paper in half.*
- *Wet the paper with water.*
- *Place your hands on the edges of the wet paper.*
- *Slowly push the sides of the paper toward the center.*

Results The paper has many folds.

Why? Your hands push the sides of the paper toward the center. Parts of the paper fold over so that it fits into the smaller space provided. When forces from opposite directions push against sections of the earth's crust, the compressed land is squeezed into new shapes called folds. The upper surface of this folded land has a wavelike appearance.

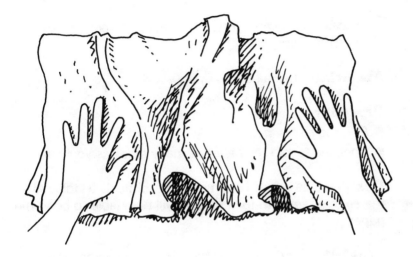

31. Easy Over?

Purpose To demonstrate the pressure required to fold the earth's crust.

Materials *1 sheet of newspaper*

Procedure
- *Fold the paper in half.*
- *Continue to fold the paper as many times as you can.*

Results The paper becomes more difficult to fold. After the sixth or seventh folding, you will be unable to bend the paper.

Why? With each folding, the amount of paper doubles. After 7 foldings there are 128 sheets. The earth's crust, like the paper, requires a small amount of pressure to fold thin, lighter layers on the surface. Tremendous amounts of pressure are required to fold over large, denser sections of land.

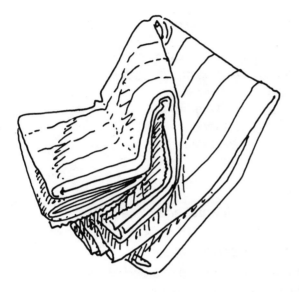

73

32. Detector

Purpose To demonstrate how a seismogram is produced.

Materials *jar with a lid, 1 qt. (1 liter)*
wide point, felt-tip pen
rubber band
masking tape
scissors
wax paper
ruler

Procedure

- *Fill the jar with water and close the lid.*
- *Cut a 6 in. × 12 in. (15 cm × 30 cm) strip of wax paper.*
- *Lay the wax paper on a table.*
- *Set the jar of water on one end of the wax paper.*
- *Attach the pen to the jar, point down, with a rubber band.*
- *Position the pen so that the felt tip touches the wax paper, then tape the pen to the jar.*
- *Hold the free end of the paper, and push the paper close to the jar.*
- *Quickly and with force pull the paper straight out from under the jar.*

Results The pen marks a line on the paper as the paper moves from under the stationary jar.

Why? Inertia is the resistance to a change in motion. Inertia increases with mass. The mass of the water-filled jar is great, and thus the inertia of the jar holds it steady while the paper moves out from under it. A seismograph has a suspended mass that holds steady, while the stand to which it is attached moves when vibrated. A pen is attached to the stationary mass with its point lightly touching the stand. Vibrations move the stand but not the pen, so the pen draws a line back and forth on the vibrating stand. A wavy line would be recorded if during an earthquake a sheet of paper was pulled slowly between the pen and the vibrating stand. This written record is called a seismogram. The line drawn by your homemade seismograph is straight because the table on which the jar sat was not vibrating. Straight-line seismograms indicated the absence of earthquakes.

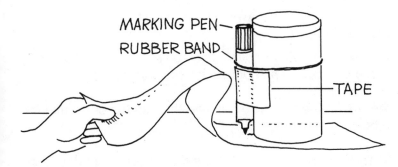

MARKING PEN

RUBBER BAND

TAPE

33. Slower

Purpose To determine why seismic waves move slowly through sand.

Materials *paper towel*
paper core from roll of paper towels
uncooked rice
rubber band

Procedure

- *Cover the end of the paper core with one paper towel sheet.*
- *Secure the paper towel to the tube with the rubber band.*
- *Fill the tube with rice.*
- *Use your fingers to push down on the rice. Try to push the rice down and out through the paper towel.*

Results The rice is not pushed through the bottom of the tube. The rice moves very little.

Why? Sand particles, like the rice, move in all directions when pushed. Vibrations from seismic waves move more slowly through sand because the forward energy of the wave moves in different directions as the sand particles move outward in all directions.

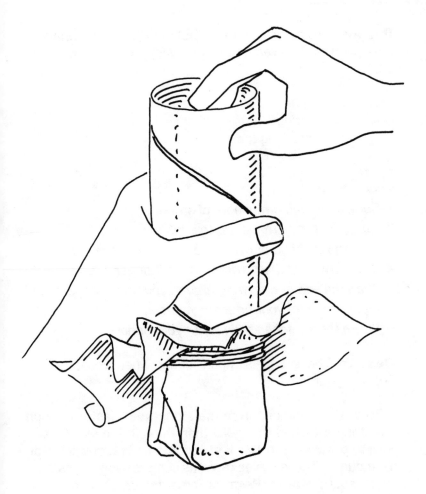

34. Quick

Purpose To determine the effect of different materials on the speed of p-waves (primary waves) produced by earthquakes.

Materials *ruler*
string
masking tape
scissors

Procedure

- *Cut a 30 in. (60 cm) length of string.*
- *Tape one end of the string to a table.*
- *Hold the free end of the string and stretch the string.*
- *Strum the stretched string with your finger. Listen.*
- *Wrap the end of the string around your index finger.*
- *Place the tip of your finger in your ear.*
- *Strum the stretched string with your fingers.*

Results The sound is much louder when you put your finger in your ear.

Why? The vibrations from the string travel faster through the string attached to a solid than through the air. Primary waves, *p-waves*, are the first recorded vibrations from an earthquake. These waves travel as compression waves similar to sound waves. P-waves move faster when traveling through dense materials—materials that have their molecules close together. The speed of p-waves gives clues to the density of the materials through which they travel.

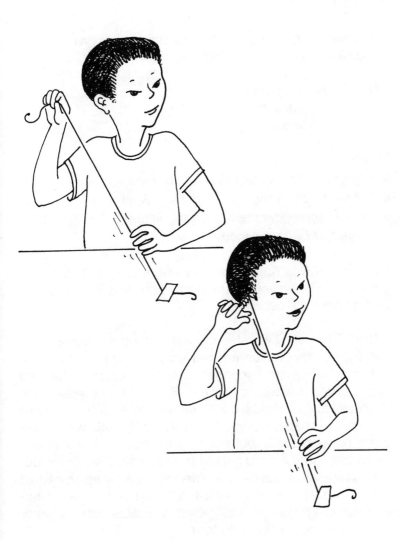

79

35. Ripples

Purpose To demonstrate how seismic waves give clues to the content of the earth's interior.

Materials *bowl, 2 qt. (2 liter)*
glass soft-drink bottle
pencil

Procedure
- *Fill the bowl about one-half full with water.*
- *Set the bottle in the center of the bowl of water.*
- *Tap the surface of the water several times near the side of the bowl with a pencil.*

Results Waves ripple out from where the pencil touches the water. The waves hit the bottle and most are reflected back toward the pencil.

Why? The pencil vibrates the water, sending out waves of energy, but the waves are not able to move through the bottle. *S-waves* are secondary waves that arrive after the faster primary waves (p-waves). Both of these waves are produced by earthquakes. S-waves are slower and have less energy than p-waves. These less energetic waves can move through solids but not through liquids. The s-waves move through the solid part of the earth but, like the water waves hitting the bottle, are reflected back by earth's liquid core. P-waves travel through the center of the earth, but s-waves are reflected back, which indicates that the inner part of the earth is in liquid form.

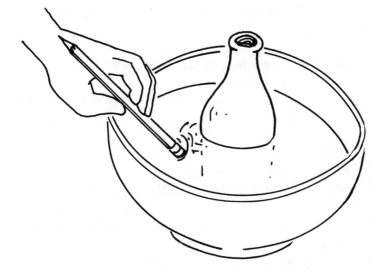

36. Flowing Ice

Purpose To determine one of the ways that glaciers might move.

Materials *access to a freezer with a wire rack*
square cake pan
a brick, or any object of comparable size and weight

Procedure

- *Fill the cake pan with water.*
- *Place the pan in the freezer until the water is frozen solid.*
- *Remove the ice from the pan and set the ice block on the wire rack in the freezer.*
- *Lay the brick on top of the ice block.*
- *Observe the bottom of the ice block after 24 hours.*

Results The ice moves through the spaces between the wire rack.

Why? Glaciers are large masses of ice in motion. When enough ice builds up, the pressure on the bottom layer of ice is so great that it becomes soft and pliable. The melting of ice due to pressure is called *regelation*. This softer ice moves outward like thick honey. As long as snow continues to fall on the surface, the height of the glacier remains constant and fingers of ice move out from the bottom of the mountain of ice. Some glaciers move only a few centimeters each day, while others move many meters in a single day.

Brick
Ice block

37. Spurt

Purpose To demonstrate what causes magma (liquid rock) to move.

Materials *half-empty tube of toothpaste*

Procedure
- *Hold the tube of toothpaste in your hands.*
- *With the cap screwed on tight, press against the tube with your thumbs and fingers.*
- *Move your fingers and press in different places on the tube.*

Results The paste in the tube moves out from under your fingers. Toothpaste bulges around the sides of your fingers.

Why? Liquid rock inside the earth is called *magma.* Pressure on pools of magma deep within the earth forces the molten rock toward the surface. Magma cools and hardens as it rises toward the surface. The liquid moves into the closest open space as did the toothpaste when it squeezed between and around the spaces formed by your fingers. Magma that moves up vertically into cracks in the crust and hardens is called a *dike.* When magma moves horizontally between rock layers, the solid, thin sheet of rock formed is called a *sill.* This horizontal movement of magma can also form a pool of liquid. This hardened dome-shaped pool is called a *laccolith.* As the laccolith forms, the layers of rock are pushed upward, a process similar to the rising of the toothpaste tube as the paste collected in one area.

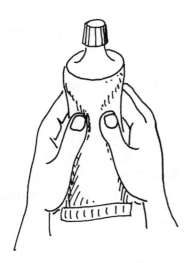

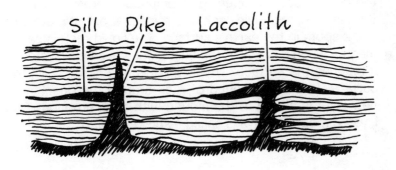

Sill   Dike   Laccolith

38. Squirt!

Purpose To demonstrate the action of a shield volcano.

Materials *pencil*
half-empty tube of toothpaste

Procedure
- *Hold the toothpaste tube in your hands.*
- *With the cap screwed on tight, push against the tube to force the toothpaste toward the capped end.*
- *Use the point of a pencil to make a hole in the tube near the cap.*

Results The toothpaste slowly emerges from the hole and flows down the side of the tube.

Why? The pressure from your fingers forces the liquid toothpaste out the opening. Tremendous pressure within the earth forces liquid rock called *magma* out of cracks or weak spots in the earth's surface. The liquid rock is called magma when it is within the earth, but it is called *lava* once it reaches the surface. The lava cools and hardens on the surface, forming a mound of rock around the opening. A new layer is added to the mound with each eruption. This layered mound of lava is called a *shield volcano.*

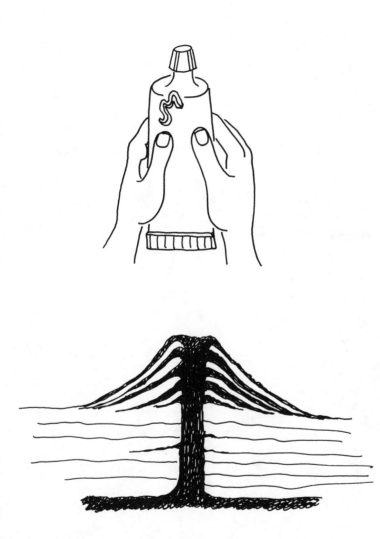

IV

Erosion

39. Rusty Rock

Purpose To demonstrate how oxygen causes a rock to crumble.

Materials *steel wool without soap (found in paint department)*
saucer

Procedure
- *Use a piece of steel wool about the size of a lemon.*
- *Moisten the steel wool with water and place it on the saucer.*
- *Allow it to sit in the saucer for 3 days.*
- *Pick up the steel wool after 3 days and rub it between your fingers.*

Caution: Steel wool can give splinters. You may want to wear a rubber glove.

Results Parts of the steel wool seem to have turned into a red powder.

Why? Oxygen combines with the iron in the steel wool pad, forming iron oxide or rust. Rocks with streaks of yellow, orange, or reddish-brown usually contain iron. The iron at the surface of the rock forms iron oxide when exposed to moist air and eventually crumbles away as did the steel wool.

Steel Wool Pad

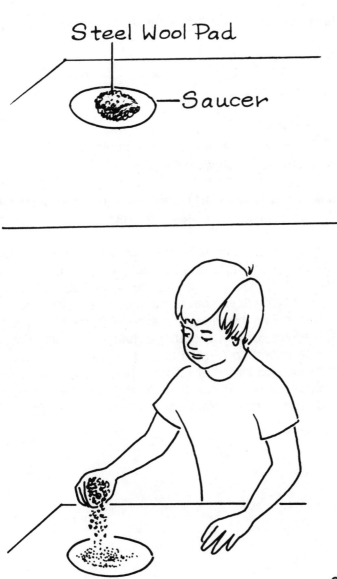

—Saucer

40. Rock Eater

Purpose To demonstrate the effect of acid on statues.

Materials *chalk*
vinegar
glass

Procedure
- *Fill a glass one-quarter full with vinegar.*
- *Add a piece of chalk to the glass.*

Results Bubbles start rising from the chalk. Small pieces start to break off, and finally the chalk totally breaks apart.

Why? Vinegar is an acid and acids slowly react chemically with the chalk. The piece of chalk is made of limestone, a mineral that quickly changes into new substances when touched by an acid. One of the new substances is the gas seen rising in the vinegar, which is carbon dioxide gas. Acids affect all minerals, but the change is usually slow. The slow deterioration of statues and building fronts is due to the weak acid rain that falls on the statue. If the stone is limestone or has limestone in it, the deterioration is more rapid. Some stones are more resistant to the attack acid.

41. Rub Away

Purpose To demonstrate how rocks change into sand and thin soil.

Materials *writing paper*
pencil with eraser

Procedure

- *Write your name on the paper with the pencil.*
- *Rub the eraser back and forth over the writing.*

Results The writing is removed and small particles are left on the paper.

Why? Graphite is a mineral found in many rocks. Pencil erasers are made of high-friction materials. Pushing this material across the soft graphite markings left by the pencil rubs the particles of graphite and some of the paper off. When wind blows sand particles against rocks, the grinding of the sand against the rock acts like the eraser and removes small pieces of the rock. Over a period of time, more and more of the rock is rubbed away, and instead of a solid rock, only sand and thin soil are left.

95

42. Shaping

Purpose To demonstrate the shaping of the land by abrasion.

Materials *fingernail file*
a six-sided pencil

Procedure
- *Rub the file back and forth across the ridges on the pencil.*
- *Observe the surface of the pencil.*

Results The ridge of the pencil is cut down.

Why? The file has a rough, grainy surface. Tiny pieces are cut from the pencil as the file moves back and forth across it. Surfaces can be pitted and polished by sand grains carried by wind. The grains of sand act like the file as they strike and cut away surfaces. This type of erosion is called *abrasion*.

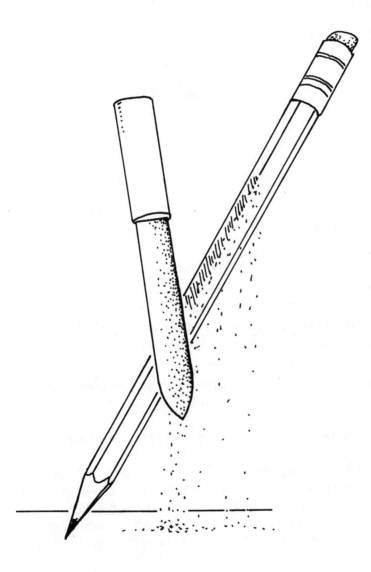

97

43. Run Off

Purpose To demonstrate how rain affects topsoil.

Materials *dirt*
red powdered tempera paint
measuring spoon, teaspoon (5 ml)
funnel
coffee filter paper
wide-mouthed jar, 1 qt. (1 liter)
measuring cup, 1 cup (250 ml)
stirring spoon

Procedure

- *Add ¼ teaspoon (1.25 ml) of red tempera paint to ¼ cup (75 ml) of dirt. Mix thoroughly.*
- *Set the funnel in the jar.*
- *Place the coffee filter inside the funnel.*
- *Pour the colored sand into the paper filter.*
- *Add ¼ cup (75 ml) of water to the funnel.*
- *Observe the water dripping into the jar.*
- *Pour this water out of the jar and add another ¼ cup (75 ml) of water to the funnel.*

Results The liquid dripping out of the funnel is red.

Why? The red paint represents nutrients in topsoil that are soluble in water. Nutrients dissolve in rainwater and feed the plants growing in the soil. If the rain is too heavy, the water runs across the land, taking the dissolved nutrients with it. Excessive rains can leave the topsoil lacking in necessary nutrients.

98

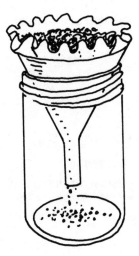

44. Wash Out

Purpose To demonstrate rock erosion due to falling water.

Materials *sponge*
bar of soap
sink with faucet

Procedure

- *Place the sponge in the sink under the faucet.*
- *Set the bar of soap on top of the sponge.*
- *Adjust the water flow from the faucet so that a medium stream of water hits the center of the soap.*
- *Allow the water to run for 60 minutes.*

Results An indentation forms in the soap where the water hits it.

Why? The falling water hits against the soap, knocking tiny particles free. A hole would form in the bar if the bar were left under the running water long enough. (Do *not* do this, since it is a waste of water!) The time it would take to form this hole depends on the hardness and solubility of the bar of soap. Eventually the entire soap bar would dissolve and wash away. Rocks at the bottom of waterfalls are slowly being washed away. These rocks are much harder than the bar of soap and are not very soluble in water, but the constant hitting of the water against the surface of the rocks slowly wears away the rocks.

45. Speedy

Purpose To demonstrate how the speed of running water affects erosion.

Materials *pencil*
paper cup
drinking straw
modeling clay
cardboard about 1 ft. (30 cm) square
dirt
1 gallon (4 liter) jar filled with water

Procedure

Note: This is an outdoor activity.

- *Use the pencil to make a hole in the side of the paper cup near the bottom rim.*
- *Cut the straw in half and insert one of the pieces in the hole in the cup.*
- *Use the clay to form a seal around the hole.*
- *Lay the cardboard on the ground and raise one end about 2 in. (5 cm) by putting dirt under the edge of the cardboard.*
- *Cover the cardboard with a thin layer of dirt.*
- *Set the cup on the raised end of the dirt with the straw pointing downhill.*
- *Hold your finger over the end of the straw as you fill the cup with water.*
- *Open the straw and observe the movement of the water.*
- *Clean the cardboard and cover it again with dirt.*
- *Raise the end of the cardboard about 6 in. (15 cm).*
- *Place the cup at the top of the incline.*

102

- *Cover the straw with your finger as you fill the cup with water.*
- *Release the straw and observe the water movement.*

Results Dirt is washed down the incline by the running water. More dirt is washed away when the slope of the cardboard is increased.

Why? As the slope increases, the water flows more quickly. The energy of the flowing water increases with speed. Moving water hits against the dirt and pushes it forward. The faster the water moves, the more energy it has, and thus the more dirt it pushes forward.

Paper cup
Clay
Drinking straw

46. Wander

Purpose To determine why streams are not always straight.

Materials *paper cup*
pencil
drinking straw
modeling clay
cardboard about 1 ft. (30 cm) square
dirt
rocks
1 gallon (4 liter) jug filled with water

Procedure
Note: This is an outdoor activity.

- *Use the pencil to make a hole in the side of the paper cup near the bottom rim.*
- *Cut the straw in half and insert one of the pieces in the hole in the cup.*
- *Use the clay to form a seal around the hole.*
- *Lay the cardboard on the ground and raise one end about 2 in. (5 cm) by putting dirt under the edge of the cardboard.*
- *Cover the cardboard with a thin layer of dirt.*
- *Set the cup on the raised end of the dirt with the straw pointing downhill.*
- *Push one rock into the soil directly in front of the straw.*
- *Continue to fill the cup with water until the water cuts a definite path in the dirt.*
- *Change the direction of the stream by placing rocks in the path of the water.*

104

Results A winding stream is cut through the dirt.

Why? Obstacles that cannot be moved by the water change the direction of the stream. Water is routed around the rocks as it is by rocks in streams. Water moves in the direction of least resistance, and the soft soil is easily moved. The shape of waterways is altered by obstacles such as rocks and materials that cannot be moved or dissolved easily by the moving water.

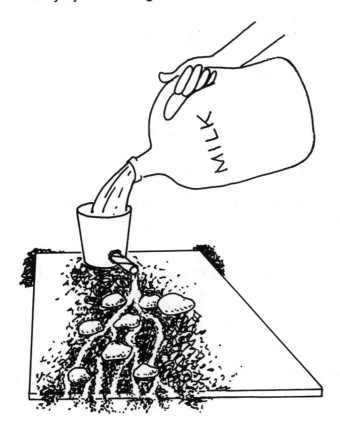

47. Fly Away

Purpose To determine how moisture affects land erosion.

Materials *paper hole punch*
sheet of paper
shallow baking pan
bowl of water

Purpose

- *Cut about 50 paper circles from the paper with the paper hole punch.*
- *Place the paper circles in the pan at one end.*
- *Blow across the paper circles.*
- *Wet your fingers in the bowl of water and sprinkle the water over the paper circles. You want the paper to be damp.*
- *Blow across the paper circles again.*

Results The dry paper particles easily move to the opposite end of the pan and some fly out of the pan. The wet paper does not move easily.

Why? Loose, lightweight particles can be picked up by the wind and carried for long distances. Flyaway surface particles that are easily supported by the wind are commonly found in deserts and along shorelines. The damp paper circles stick together and are too heavy for your breath to lift. Damp land areas and those covered by vegetation are not as easily eroded by the wind, because, like the damp paper, the materials are too heavy to be lifted by the wind.

48. Crack-Up

Purpose To determine if freezing water causes rock movement.

Materials *drinking straw*
modeling clay
freezer
glass of water

Procedure

- *Place one end of the straw into the glass of water.*
- *Fill the straw by sucking the water into it.*
- *Hold your tongue over one end to prevent the water from escaping while you insert a clay plug into the open end of the straw.*
- *Remove your tongue and plug the end with clay.*
- *Lay the straw in the freezer for 3 hours.*
- *Remove the straw and observe the ends.*

Results One of the clay plugs has been pushed out of the straw and a column of ice is extending past the end of the straw.

Why? Water, unlike most substances, expands when it freezes. When water gets into cracks in and around rocks, it can actually move or break the rock when it freezes. The expansion of the freezing water is enough to push apart weak points in the rocks. This is the main cause of potholes in the streets.

109

49. Pile Up

Purpose To demonstrate the formation of sand dunes.

Materials *drinking straw*
shallow baking pan
flour

Procedure

- *Cover the bottom of the baking pan with a thin, flat layer of flour.*
- *Use the straw to direct your exhaled breath toward the edge of the flour.*

Results The flour moves away from the end of the straw in a semicircular pattern. The flour piles up close to the end of the straw.

Why? The moving air leaving the straw has kinetic energy (energy of motion). The flour particles are small enough to be lifted by the moving air and carried forward. Some of the smaller particles move farther away, but most lose energy and fall, forming a mound near the end of the straw. As this mound builds, it blocks the movement of even the smaller flour particles that would have traveled farther. This demonstrates the formation of sand dunes.

50. Shake-Up

Purpose To determine the effect of motion on erosion.

Materials *2 equal-sized pieces of colored hard candy*
2 equal-sized jars with lids
measuring cup, 1 cup (250 ml)

Procedure

- *Pour one cup of water into each jar.*
- *Add one piece of candy to each jar and close the jar with a lid.*
- *Place one jar where it will not be disturbed for 2 days.*
- *Choose a place for the second jar that allows you to shake the jar often for 1 day.*

Results Shaking the jar dissolves more of the candy.

Why? Both candy pieces are soluble in the water. Vigorous movement causes the water to rub against the candy, knocking off small pieces that dissolve in the water. Hard mud balls in a pond would dissolve slowly, as did the candy in the undisturbed jar. A similar mud ball in a fast-moving stream would dissolve more quickly because, like the candy in the jar that was shaken, it would have pieces knocked off by the moving water.

113

51. Rock Bridge

Purpose To demonstrate how natural bridges stand.

Materials *books*
2 flat chairs the same height

Procedure

- *Move the chairs about 12 in. (30 cm) apart.*
- *Lay one book on each chair with the edge of the books even with the edges of the chairs.*
- *Stack books on top of each other so that each book extends farther over the edge of the chair.*
- *Continue stacking the books until one book overlaps the stack from both chairs to form a bridge.*

Results No part of the bottom books overlaps the edge of the chair. Each book above the bottom book extends over the chair's edge until the top book is totally over the edges of the chairs.

Why? All objects behave as if their weight is located in one spot called the *center of gravity.* The book bridge balances because the center of gravity of each side of the bridge is over a chair. In nature, natural rock bridges are formed by weathering and erosional processes. These bridges balance because the particles making up the bridge overlap in such a way that they place the center of gravity of the structure over the supporting sides.

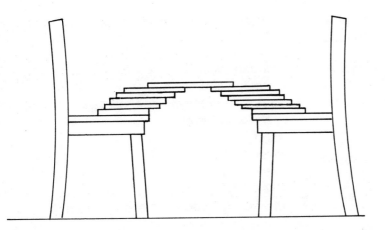

52. Up and Down

Purpose To determine how erosion causes mountains to rise.

Materials wooden block 2 in. × 4 in. × 2 in. (5 cm × 10
cm × 5 cm)
see-through container about twice as large as
the wooden block
sand
masking tape
marking pen
ruler
measuring spoon, tablespoon (15 ml)

Procedure

- Fill the container about one-half full with water.
- Place a piece of tape down the side of the container
- Start at the top of the tape and mark it off in centimeters.
- Place a piece of tape down the side of the wooden block and mark it off in centimeters.
- Place the wooden block in the container of water.
- Pour one spoon of sand on top of the block.
- Observe the water level on the block and in the container.
- Use the spoon to scrape the sand from the top of the block into the water.
- Observe the water level on the block and in the container.

Results The wooden block floats higher in the water when the sand is removed, but the water level in the container stays the same.

116

Why? The water level is forced upward by the weight of the sand and the wooden block. Removing the sand from the block decreases the weight of the block, allowing it to float higher in the water. Moving the sand from the block to the water does not change the total weight in the bowl, so the water level in the container remains the same. This same balance is achieved by the erosion of mountains. The weight of the mountain decreases and it floats higher on the mantle as materials are washed into the ocean. The weight of the added sediment along the seacoast causes the crust below it to sink. The mountain rises and the ocean crust sinks. This equal up-and-down movement of the earth's crust is called *isostasy*.

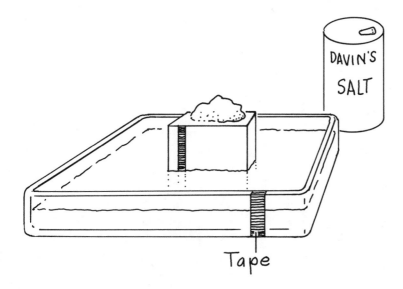

Tape

V

Atmosphere

53. Spacey

Purpose To demonstrate that air takes up space.

Materials *clear drinking glass*
bowl, 2 qt. (2 liter)
small cork

Procedure
- *Fill the bowl one-half full with water.*
- *Float the cork on the water's surface.*
- *Hold the glass above the floating cork.*
- *Press the open mouth of the glass down into the water.*

Results The surface of the water with the floating cork is pushed down.

Why? The pocket of air inside the glass prevents the water from entering the glass, so the water with the floating cork is forced down below the level of the water outside the glass.

121

54. Tip

Purpose To determine if air has weight.

Materials *thick cord, 2 ft. (60 cm)*
balloon, 9 in. (23 cm)
yardstick (meter stick)
string
modeling clay
masking tape
straight pin

Procedure

■ *Place a piece of clay on one end of the yardstick.*

■ *Inflate the balloon to its maximum size and use string to attach it to the end of the yardstick opposite the clay.*

■ *Place a small strip of tape about 1 in. (2.5 cm) long on the side of the inflated balloon, near the neck.*

■ *Use the ribbon to suspend the yardstick. Move the ribbon so that the stick balances.*

■ *Attach the top end of the ribbon to the side of a table or door frame so that the yardstick hangs freely.*

■ *Slowly insert the pin through the strip of tape and into the balloon. Remove the pin.*

Results The end of the stick with the clay tips downward as the air leaves the balloon.

Why? Air has weight. As the air leaves the balloon, the side of the stick with the balloon becomes lighter. The earth is surrounded by an ocean of air, which weighs so much that every square inch of the earth supports about 14.7 pounds of air (1 square centimeter supports 1 kg of air).

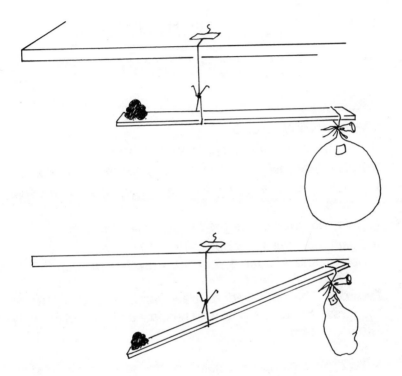

55. Straw Drill

Purpose To demonstrate the strength of air.

Materials *2 plastic drinking straws*
1 raw potato

Procedure

- *Place the potato on a table.*
- *Hold the straw at the top, leaving the top open.*
- *Raise the straw about 4 in. (10 cm) above the potato.*
- *Quickly and with force stick the end of the straw into the potato.*
- *Hold your thumb over the top of the second straw.*
- *Again raise the straw about 4 in. (10 cm) above the potato, and with force stick the straw into the potato.*

Results The open-ended straw bends, and very little of the straw enters the potato. The closed straw cuts deeply into the potato.

Why? Air is composed mainly of the gases nitrogen, oxygen, and carbon dioxide. These gases are invisible, but the results of their presence can be observed. Fast-moving air (wind) can apply enough pressure to destroy large buildings. The trapped air inside the straw makes the straw strong enough to break through the skin of the potato. The push of the air against the inside of the straw prevents it from bending. The pressure of the air increases as the plug of potato enters and compresses the air.

124

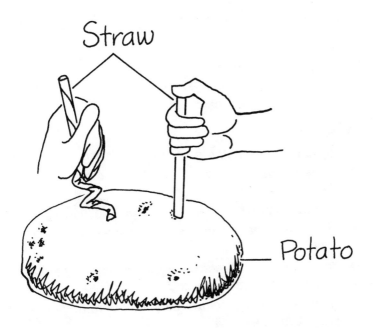

Straw

Potato

56. Cold 'n Hot

Purpose To determine how the earth's heat level remains constant.

Materials *2 thermometers*
2 plastic bags, 1 large and 1 small, with twist ties

Procedure
- *Lay one thermometer inside the small bag.*
- *Inflate the bag by blowing into it, then close the end with the twist tie.*
- *Put the inflated bag inside the larger plastic bag.*
- *Inflate the large bag with air and close the end with the twist tie.*
- *Place the bag in direct sunlight, and lay the second thermometer next to the bag.*
- *Observe the temperature reading of both thermometers after 30 minutes.*
- *Move the bag and free thermometer to a dark closet.*
- *Observe the temperature reading on both thermometers after 30 minutes.*

Results In the sunlight, the thermometer reading inside the bag was higher, and it changed more slowly after being placed in the dark area.

Why? The double layer of air inside the bag acts like a greenhouse, as does the atmosphere around the earth. Both envelopes of air allow radiant energy from the sun to enter, and the resulting heat energy is trapped. Sunlight enters the earth's atmosphere, and this radiation is absorbed by plants

126

and soil that change it into heat energy. Heat energy is radiated from the earth's surface toward space, but the gases in the atmosphere absorb and reradiate the heat back toward the earth. The air inside the plastic bags similarly reradiates the heat, thus keeping the temperature inside warmer. The earth's atmosphere, like the air bags, acts as an insulator, holding on to the heat absorbed from the sun during the daytime. This trapped energy inside the atmosphere is constantly being moved from one place to the other, which prevents extreme differences in day and night temperatures. Without this protective layer of air, the earth would get very hot during the day and very cold at night.

57. Increasing

Purpose To determine how temperature affects air pressure.

Materials *freezer*
glass soft-drink bottle
balloon, 9 in. (23 cm)

Procedure
- *Place the open bottle in the freezer for 1 hour.*
- *Remove the bottle from the freezer.*
- *Stretch the opening of the balloon over the mouth of the bottle.*
- *Allow the bottle to stand at room temperature for 15 minutes.*

Results The balloon partially inflates.

Why? The air inside the bottle contracts when cooled. This allows more air to enter the bottle. The balloon seals the bottle; as the air inside heats, it expands and moves into the balloon, causing it to inflate. Air in the atmosphere contracts and expands as it is cooled and heated as did the air in the bottle. Expanding warm air rises and decreases atmospheric pressure; the pressure increases as the air cools and descends. Temperature is just one factor that affects atmospheric pressure, but a rise in pressure is a good indication that nice weather can be expected.

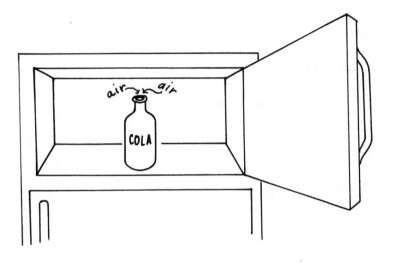

129

58. Up Draft

Purpose To determine the effect that temperature has on air movement.

Materials *ruler*
desk lamp
tissue paper
thread
scissors
cellophane tape

Procedure

- *Cut a 2 in. (6 cm) diameter spiral from the tissue paper.*
- *Cut a piece of thread 6 in. (15 cm) long.*
- *Tape one end of the piece of thread to the center of the paper spiral.*
- *Turn the desk lamp so that the light points upward.*
- *Holding the end of the thread, position the paper spiral about 4 in. (10 cm) above the light.*

Results The paper spiral twirls.

Why? The energy from the light heats the air above it. The air molecules move faster and farther apart as they absorb energy. The separation of the molecules makes the air lighter and it rises upward. Cooler air rushes in to take the place of the warmer rising air. As long as the lamp is on, warm air rises and cooler air moves in to take its place producing air movements called convection currents.

131

59. Breezes

Purpose To determine the cause of land and sea breezes.

Materials *ruler*
2 thermometers
2 glasses large enough to hold the
thermometers
desk lamp
dirt

Procedure

- *Pour 2 in. (6 cm) of water into a glass.*
- *Pour 2 in. (6 cm) of dirt into the second glass.*
- *Place a thermometer in each glass.*
- *Set the glasses together on a table and allow them to stand for 30 minutes before recording the reading on each thermometer.*
- *Position the lamp so that the light evenly hits both glasses.*
- *Record the temperature on each thermometer after 1 hour.*
- *Turn the light off.*
- *Record the temperature on each thermometer after 1 hour.*

Results The temperature of the dirt increases more than the water, and the dirt cools faster than does the water.

Why? The difference in the time it takes land and water to change temperature affects the movement of air above it. During the day, the land heats more quickly than the ocean. Hot air above the land rises, and cooler air above the water rushes in to take the place of the rising warm air. This air movement is called a sea breeze. At night the land cools faster than the water. The hotter air above the water rises, and the cooler air above the land rushes toward the ocean. This is called a land breeze.

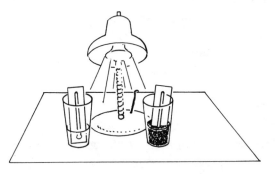

SEA BREEZES

LAND BREEZES

60. How Fast?

Purpose To demonstrate how wind speed is measured.

Materials *pencil*
4 small paper drinking cups, 5 oz. (150 ml)
2 drinking straws
straight pin
masking tape

Procedure

- *Cross and tape the drinking straws in the center.*
- *Insert the straight pin through the overlapping straws.*
- *Use the pencil to punch one hole near the rim of each cup.*
- *Insert the end of a straw in the hole of each cup.*
- *Tape each cup to the straw so that it is horizontal.*
- *Stick the pin into the eraser of the pencil.*
- *Hold the pencil upright and position the cups about 12 in. (30 cm) from your face.*
- *Gently blow toward the cups.*
- *Now blow as hard as you can toward the cups.*

Results A gently breeze causes the cups to spin slowly, and a fast, stronger wind causes the cups to spin quickly.

Why? Your whirling cups are called a Robinson anemometer. An anemometer is an instrument that tells how fast the wind blows. Moving air fills the cups, causing them to spin. The speed of the wind hitting the cups is determined by the number of turns per minute made by the cups.

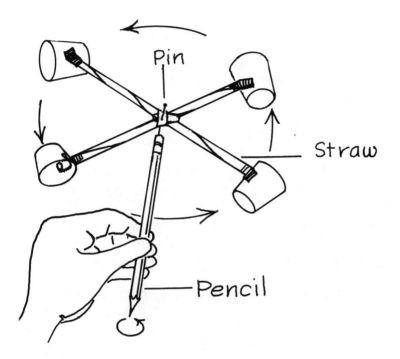

Pin

Straw

Pencil

135

61. Which Way?

Purpose To determine why the air is cooler in the winter.

Materials *flashlight*
1 sheet of dark paper

Procedure
- *In a dark room, hold the flashlight about 6 in. (15 cm) directly above the dark paper.*
- *Observe the size and shape of the light pattern formed.*
- *Tilt the flashlight and observe the light pattern again.*

Results The light coming straight down produces a small, bright circle. Slanting the flashlight produces a larger, less bright pattern on the paper.

Why? In the winter, the sun does not heat the earth as much as it does during other times of the year. The position of the sun in the sky during the winter is not as high in the sky as during other seasons. Winter sunlight comes in at an angle, like the light from the slanted flashlight. This light travels through more of the atmosphere and covers a large area on the surface where it strikes. These slanted rays are spread over a larger area and do not heat as much as when the rays shine straight down.

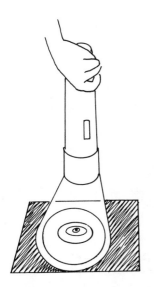 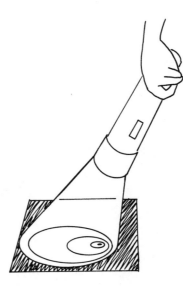

137

VI

Weather

62. Up and Down

Purpose To demonstrate how a thermometer works.

Materials *outdoor thermometer*
cup
ice cube

Procedure

- *Hold the bulb of the thermometer between your fingers.*
- *Observe the level of the liquid in the thermometer.*
- *Fill the cup with water. Add an ice cube and stir.*
- *Place the bulb of the thermometer in the cold water.*
- *Observe the level of the liquid in the thermometer.*

Results Holding the bulb between your fingers caused the liquid in the thermometer to rise. The liquid lowered in the thermometer column when the bulb was placed in cold water.

Why? Heat from your fingers increases the temperature of the liquid inside the thermometer. As the liquid is heated, it expands and rises in the thermometer tube. The cold water removes heat from the liquid in the thermometer. As the liquid cools, it contracts and moves down the tube. Outdoor thermometers are used to measure the temperature of air. Any increase or decrease in the heat content of air causes the liquid inside the thermometer to expand or contract, thus indicating the temperature of the surrounding air.

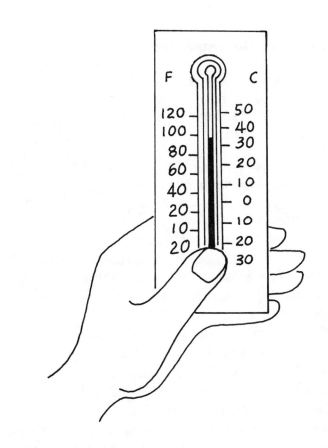

141

63. Barometer

Purpose To demonstrate how air pressure is measured.

Materials *small baby food jar*
wide-mouthed jar, 1 qt. (1 liter)
2 balloons, 9 in. (23 cm)
scissors
glue
flat toothpick
2 rubber bands

Procedure
- *Cut the top from one of the balloons.*
- *Stretch the bottom section of the cut balloon over the mouth of the small jar and secure with a rubber band.*
- *Glue the large end of the toothpick to the rubber lid and allow it to dry.*
- *Place the small jar inside the wide-mouthed jar.*
- *Cut the bottom from the second balloon and stretch it over the mouth of the large jar.*
- *Secure the balloon with a rubber band.*
- *Tie the neck of the balloon.*
- *Observe the toothpick on the small jar as you pull up and push down on the balloon stretched across the large jar.*

Results The toothpick moves up and down.

Why? Pressing down on the balloon causes the pressure of the air inside the large jar to increase. The compressed air pushes against the rubber stretched across the small jar. When this rubber lid is pushed down, the attached toothpick

142

points upward. Pulling up on the balloon stem allows the air in the jar to spread out, which decreases the pressure in the jar. With less pressure pushing on the small jar's lid, the air inside the small jar expands, causing the lid to rise and the toothpick to point down.

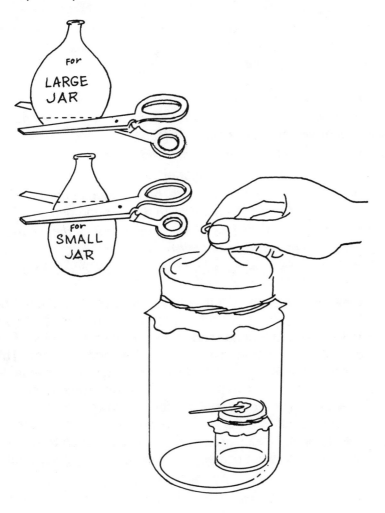

64. Cloud Watcher

Purpose To determine wind direction by use of a nephoscope.

Materials *mirror*
marking pen
compass
paper

Procedure
- *Try this experiment on different days when the sky has separate clumps of moving clouds.*
- *Lay a sheet of paper on an outside table.*
- *Place a mirror in the center of the paper.*
- *Use a compass to determine the direction of north. Mark the direction on the paper with the marking pen.*
- *Look into the mirror and watch the image of the clouds as they move cross the mirror.*
- *Record the directions that the clouds are coming from.*

Results The image of the clouds moves across the mirror.

Why? The direction and speed of surface winds are changed by obstructions such as trees and buildings. This is why meteorologists and weather forecasters seek information about wind in the upper air. The instrument that you have made is called a *nephoscope*. It allows you to observe drifting clouds in order to determine the direction of wind in the upper air. Winds are named for the direction they come from. A north wind comes from the north and blows south.

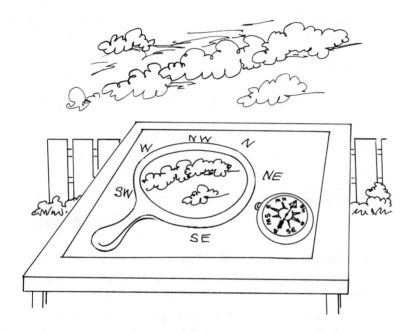

65. Wet Air

Purpose To demonstrate the use of hair in measuring humidity.

Materials *glue*
marker
large glass jar
pencil
cellophane tape
flat toothpick
straight strand of hair about 5 in. (12 cm) long

Procedure

- *Use a small piece of tape to secure one end of the strand of hair to the center of the toothpick.*
- *Color the pointed end of the toothpick with the marker.*
- *Tape the free end of the hair strand to the center of the pencil.*
- *Place the pencil across the mouth of the jar with the toothpick hanging inside the jar. If the toothpick does not hang horizontally, add a drop of glue to the light end to balance the toothpick.*
- *Place the jar where it will be undisturbed.*
- *Observe the directions that the toothpick points for one week.*

Results The toothpick changes direction.

Why? You have made a hair *hygrometer*. Hygrometers are instruments used to measure humidity, the amount of water in air. The hair stretches when the humidity increases; with a lower humidity, the hair shrinks. The stretching and shrinking of the hair pulls on the toothpick, causing it to move.

146

66. Wet Bulb

Purpose To determine how a psychrometer measures relative humidity.

Materials two thermometers
1 cotton ball
fan

Procedure
- *Place both thermometers on a table.*
- *Record the temperature on both thermometers.*
- *Wet the cotton ball with water and place it over the bulb of one of the thermometers.*
- *Place the fan so that it blows across the bulbs of both thermometers.*
- *Record the temperature of the two bulbs after 5 minutes.*

Results The thermometer that has its bulb covered with wet cotton has a lower temperature.

Why? The wet bulb thermometer is cooled as the water evaporates from the cotton. The faster the water evaporates, the lower the temperature on this thermometer. The dry bulb thermometer records the air temperature. A low humidity (amount of water in the air) is indicated by a large difference between the wet and dry bulb reading. The instrument that measures air humidity by comparing the temperatures on a wet and dry bulb thermometer is called a *psychrometer.*

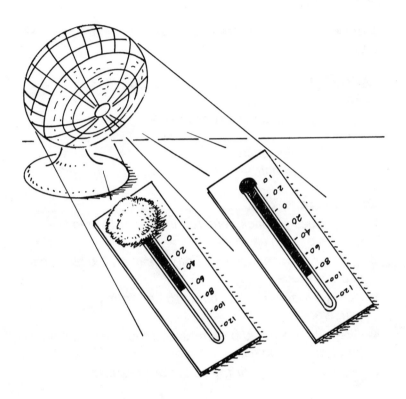

149

67. Soggy

Purpose To demonstrate the use of salt in measuring humidity.

Materials *measuring spoon, teaspoon (5 ml)*
table salt
black construction paper
scissors
2 saucers
pencil

Procedure

- *Cut a piece of black construction paper to fit in the bottom of both saucers.*
- *Sprinkle 1/2 teaspoon (1.25 ml) of salt on the black paper in each saucer.*
- *Hold your mouth about 6 in. (15 cm) from one of the saucers.*
- *Direct your exhaled breath toward the salt in one saucer for about 2 minutes.*
- *Use the pencil to stir the salt in both saucers.*

Results The salt that was breathed on forms clumps when stirred, while the salt crystals in the other dish remain separate.

Why? Exhaled breath contains water vapor. The water causes the salt crystals to stick together. Air that contains a large amount of water causes salt to become soggy. A high humidity (amount of water in the air) is indicated when salt is difficult to shake from saltshakers.

151

68. Crackle

Purpose To demonstrate how static electricity can be used to indicate humidity levels.

Materials *clean, dry, oil-free hair*
plastic comb

Procedure

- *This experiments needs to be performed on several different days and the results noted.*
- *Be sure that your hair is clean, dry, and oil-free.*
- *Briskly comb your hair.*

Results On some days, a crackling sound is heard as you comb your hair and on other days no sound is heard.

Why? Electrons are rubbed from the hair and onto the comb. Sound waves are produced when the electrons jump from the comb through the air and back to the hair. The crackling sound is heard best when the air is cool and dry and not heard at all when the air is warm and wet. Wet air contains many molecules of water that provide stepping stones for the electrons to use when they move through the air. As the air becomes dryer, the number of water molecules decreases, so the electrons have a longer distance to jump when returning from the comb to the hair. The electrons clump together until the combined amount of their energy is great enough to move them across the span. The movement of these groups of electrons through the air produces the crackling sound.

153

69. More or Less

Purpose To determine the effects of surface temperature on dew formation.

Materials *clock*
glass bottle
jar large enough for the bottle to fit inside
ice
paper towels

Procedure

■ *Wrap your hands around the bottle and hold it for 2 minutes. You want as much of your skin to touch the glass as possible.*

■ *Exhale on the outside of the bottle.*

■ *Observe the surface of the bottle.*

■ *Fill the jar one-half full with water and add 4 to 5 ice cubes.*

■ *Set the bottle in the icy water for 2 minutes.*

■ *Remove the bottle and dry the outside with a paper towel.*

■ *Exhale on the outside of the bottle.*

Results The surface of the warm bottle clouds over when the exhaled breath touches it, but the cloud quickly disappears, leaving a dry surface. The cloud formed on the cold bottle by the exhaled breath turns into tiny drops of water. The entire surface of the cold bottle clouds if the humidity of the air is high.

Why? Water vapor from your exhaled breath condenses (changes into a liquid) on the surface of both bottles. The warm surface supplies energy for the tiny water droplets to quickly evaporate (change into a vapor). The tiny droplets on the cold surface group together, forming large drops of water. Cold surfaces collect more water drops (dew) than do warmer surfaces. If the surface is too warm, water vapor in the air striking the surface will not condense at all, and if there is a collection of moisture, it quickly evaporates.

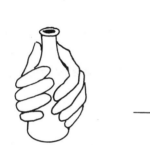 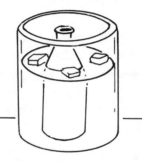

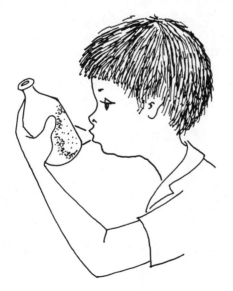

70. Cooling

Purpose To determine how color affects the dew point.

Materials *1 sheet of white construction paper*
1 sheet of black construction paper

Procedure
- *Perform this experiment on several different calm, clear nights.*
- *Just before sunset, place both sheets of paper on the ground out in the open.*
- *Check the papers every half hour for 2 hours.*

Results Dew forms first on the black paper; on some nights, dew is found *only* on the black paper.

Why? Dew forms on an object when that object cools enough to cause water vapor in the air to condense. Dark materials radiate or lose heat energy faster than do materials with a light color, so the dew point is reached faster by the black paper. On some nights, the white paper does not get cold enough for the dew to form at all.

71. Under Cover

Purpose To determine the effect of overhead covering on dew formation.

Materials *umbrella*
2 sheets of black construction paper

Procedure

- *Perform this experiment on several different calm, clear nights.*
- *Just before sunset, open the umbrella and place it on the ground.*
- *Lay one sheet of black paper under the umbrella and lay the second sheet of paper on the ground with no overhead covering.*
- *After sunset, check the papers each half hour for 2 hours.*

Results Water collects on the paper with no overhead covering, but not on the protected paper.

Why? Dew point is the temperature at which water vapor in the air condenses (changes to a liquid). The black papers cool by losing heat energy. The heat radiates (moves away) from the sheets of paper if they are not covered. The one uncovered sheet loses enough energy to cool to dew point, so water condenses on its surface. Some of the heat from the covered paper is absorbed by the umbrella and is radiated back to the paper, keeping the paper from cooling to dew point. Clouds, tree branches, and other overhead coverings can prevent dew from forming on objects beneath them.

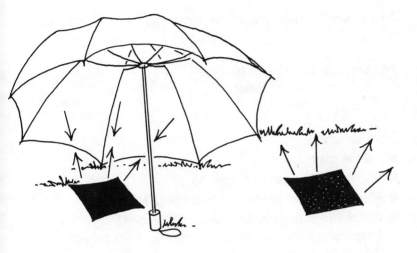

72. Dew Point

Purpose To determine the temperature at which dew forms.

Materials *drinking glass*
thermometer
ice

Procedure
- *Fill the glass with ice.*
- *Add enough water to cover the ice.*
- *Place the thermometer in the glass of icy water.*
- *Watch the outside of the glass and record the temperature when water is observed on the outside of the glass.*
- *Perform this experiment several times, selecting days that have different humidities.*

Results When the humidity is high, the water collects on the glass at a higher temperature.

Why? Water vapor in the air condenses (changes to a liquid) when it touches the cool surface of the glass. The *dew point* is the temperature at which water vapor condenses. A high dew point indicates a high humidity (amount of water in the air).

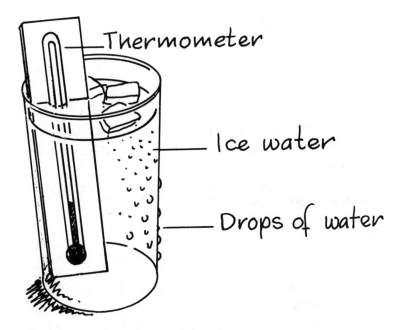

Thermometer

Ice water

Drops of water

73. Frosty

Purpose To determine how frost forms.

Materials *drinking glass*
freezer

Procedure

- *Place a drinking glass in the freezer for 30 minutes.*
- *Remove the glass and allow it to stand undisturbed for 30 seconds.*
- *Scratch the cloudy formation on the outside of the glass with your fingernail.*

Results The glass looks frosty, and a very thin layer of soft snow seems to be stuck to the outside of the glass.

Why? Frost is not frozen dew. Frost forms when water vapor changes directly to a solid. The glass is cold enough to cause the water vapor in the air to cool so quickly that it *sublimes* (changes from a gas to a solid without forming a liquid).

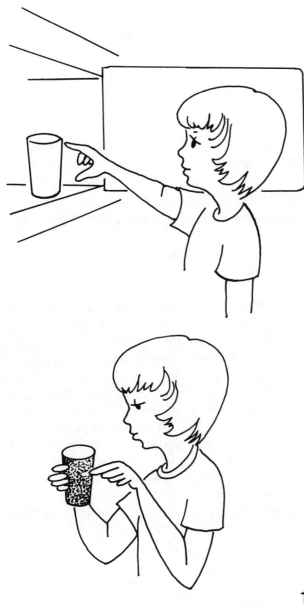

163

74. Drops

Purpose To determine how raindrops form.

Materials *jar with lid, 1 qt. (1 liter)*
ice cubes

Procedure

- *Pour enough water into the jar to cover the bottom.*
- *Turn the jar lid upside down and set it over the mouth of the jar.*
- *Put 3 to 4 ice cubes inside the lid.*
- *Observe the underside of the lid for 10 minutes.*

Results The lid looks wet, and finally water drops form on the underside of the lid.

Why? Some of the liquid water in the bottom of the jar evaporates (changes into a gas). The water vapor condenses and then changes back to a liquid when it hits the cool underside of the lid. As the amount of liquid increases, drops form on the underside of the lid. In nature, liquid water evaporates from open water areas such as streams, lakes, and oceans. This vapor rises and condenses as it hits the cooler upper air. Clouds are made of tiny drops of liquid water suspended in the air. Water drops in clouds range in size from .000079 to .0039 in. (.002 to .1 mm) in diameter. The tiny water drops join together, forming larger, heavier drops. The drops start falling as rain when air can no longer support them. Falling raindrops range in size from .24 to .79 in. (2 to 6 mm).

164

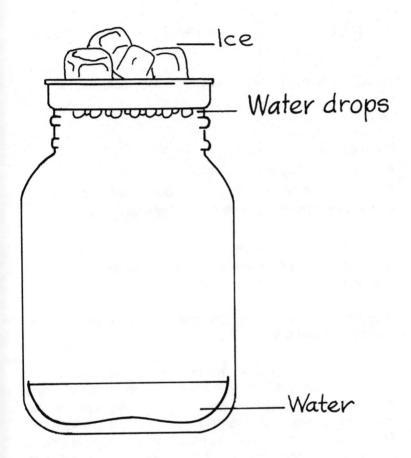

Ice

Water drops

Water

75. Bigger

Purpose To determine how tiny water droplets in clouds grow into raindrops.

Materials *plastic see-through lid (coffee can lid)*
eye dropper
pencil

Procedure
- *Fill the eye dropper with water.*
- *Hold the plastic lid in your hand, bottom side up.*
- *Squeeze as many separate drops of water as will fit on the lid.*
- *Quickly turn the lid over.*
- *Use the point of a pencil to move the tiny drops of water together.*

Results The drops leap together, forming larger drops. The large drops fall.

Why? Water molecules have an attraction for each other. This attraction is due to the fact that each molecule has a positive and a negative side. The positive side of the molecule attracts the negative side of another molecule. The tiny water droplets on the plastic lid as well as in clouds join to form larger, heavier drops, which fall. The falling drops from clouds are called raindrops.

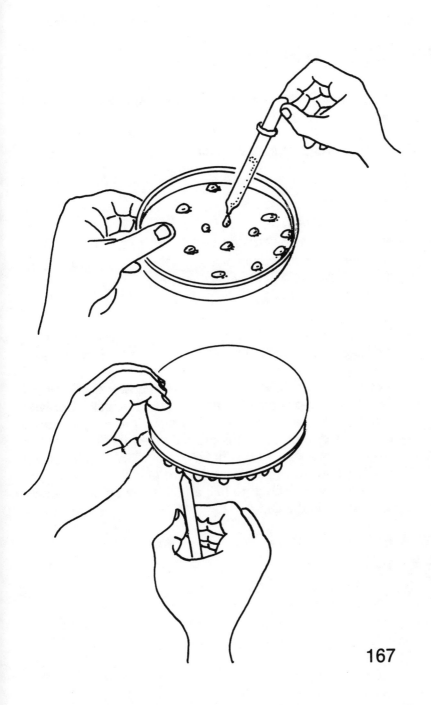

76. Rising Drops

Purpose To demonstrate how the speed and direction of air affect falling rain.

Materials *plastic beach ball*
fan

Procedure
- *Inflate the ball.*
- *Turn the fan upward and switch to high speed.*
- *Place the ball over the blowing fan.*
- *Turn the speed of the fan to low speed.*
- *Observe the movement of the ball.*

Results The ball floats above the fan when the fan is on high speed, but falls when the speed of the fan is decreased.

Why? The air above the fan is moving upward very quickly and has enough force to lift the ball. The pull of gravity prevents the ball from rising very high. In a thunderstorm, raindrops do not fall to the ground when the speed of the updraft is more than 17 mi/hr (27 km/hr). The force of the air moving upward at this speed tears apart large raindrops that are heavy enough to fall, and the tiny droplets remain suspended in the air.

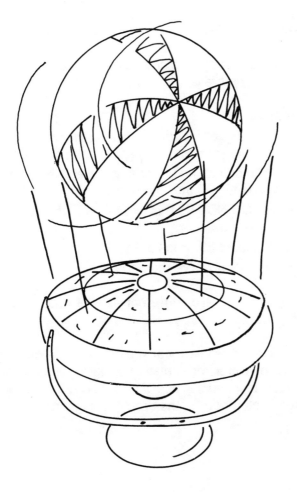

77. How Big?

Purpose To collect and compare raindrop sizes.

Materials *1 sheet of black construction paper*
umbrella

Procedure

■ *On a rainy day, stand under an umbrella while holding the sheet of black construction paper so the rain can hit it.*
Note: You can stand under any protective covering and hold the paper out into the rain.
Caution: DO NOT do this experiment when there is lightning and thunder.

■ Collect at least 20 drops of rain.

■ In a dry area, observe the paper.

Results There will be different sizes of water spots on the paper.

Why? Raindrops are not all the same size. A drop of rain is made up of water molecules clinging together. Small raindrops have fewer molecules of water, and as more molecules of water stick together, the drop gets bigger.

78. Vanishing Water

Purpose To determine why lakes dry up.

Materials 2 glass jars, one with a lid
masking tape
marking pen

Procedure

- Put a strip of tape down the side of both jars from top of to bottom.
- Fill both jars half full with water.
- Use the marking pen to mark the top of the water level on each strip of tape.
- Seal one jar with a lid and leave the second jar open.
- Allow the jars to sit undisturbed for two weeks.
- Observe the level of the water in each jar and mark the new level if there is a change.

Results The level of the water in the open jar is lower and the water level in the closed jar is unchanged. On some days, the closed jar looked cloudy, and drops of water cling to the inside of the glass.

Why? Liquid water molecules on the surface of water absorb enough energy from the surrounding air to change into a vapor. In the open jar, like any body of water exposed to the open air, water molecules on the surface vaporize and move upward into the atmosphere. As each water molecule vaporizes and leaves, the level of the water decreases. Surface water vaporized in the closed jar, but it was not able to escape. The vapor condensed (changed back into a liquid) as it hit the cool surface of the jar. The rising vapor above a lake or any body of water condenses when cooled, but the water droplets can be carried to other areas by moving wind. Lakes dry up when the evaporating surface water does not return in the form of rain.

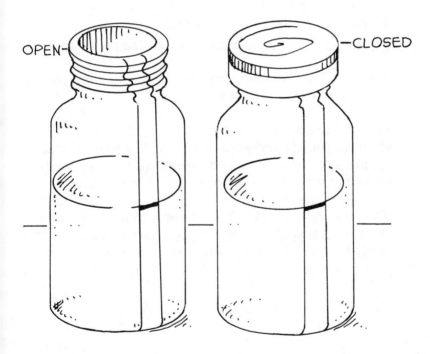

OPEN —

— CLOSED

79. Floating Flakes

Purpose To demonstrate why snowflakes float.

Materials *2 sheets of notebook paper*

Procedure
- *Crumple one of the paper sheets into a ball.*
- *Hold the flat sheet in one hand and the crumpled sheet in your other hand.*
- *Drop both sheets at the same time.*
- *Observe which sheet of paper strikes the floor first.*

Results The crumpled sheet hits the floor first; the flat sheet floats slowly downward.

Why? The downward pull of gravity is the same on both sheets of paper, but the upward force of air on each sheet is not the same. Raindrops and snowflakes are both made of water, but they have different shapes. The raindrop, like the crumpled paper, takes up a small amount of space and falls more quickly than does the flat sheet of paper, which behaves like a snowflake. The flat paper, like snowflakes, falls slowly because it has a greater exposed area and thus receives more upward force from the air.

80. Low Pressure

Purpose To demonstrate the formation and effect of low pressure.

Materials *ruler*
cellophane tape
sewing thread
2 balloons, 9 in. (23 cm)
pencil

Procedure

- *Inflate each balloon to the size of an apple and tie.*
- *Attach a 12 in. (30 cm) thread to the top of each balloon.*
- *Tape the ends of each thread to the pencil so that the balloon hang about 3 in. (8 cm) apart.*
- *Hold the pencil level with the balloons about 3 in. (8 cm) from your face.*
- *Direct your exhaled breath between the balloons.*

Results The balloons move together.

Why? The fast-moving air between the balloons reduces the air pressure on the insides of the balloons, and the air pressure on the outside pushes the balloons together. The rapidly rising air in a tornado creates a very low pressure area. Houses near a tornado have been known to explode because of the sudden reduction in pressure outside the house. The air inside the house pushes with a greater force than the air outside, forcing the walls outward.

176

177

81. Tornado

Procedure To demonstrate the appearance of a tornado.

Materials *2 plastic, 2-qt. (2-liter) soft-drink bottles*
duct tape
scissors
pencil
paper towels
ruler

Procedure

- *Fill one bottle half full with water.*
- *Cut a strip of tape about 1 in. × 2 in. (2.5 cm × 5 cm).*
- *Cover the mouth of the bottle containing water with the strip of tape.*
- *Use the pencil to punch a hole in the center of the tape. Make the hole slightly larger than the pencil.*
- *Use your fingers to smooth and secure the edges of the tape around the hole in the tape.*
- *Turn the second bottle so that the mouth of each bottle lines up.*
- *Use a paper towel to dry any moisture from the necks of the bottles.*
- *Wrap strips of tape around the necks of the bottles to secure them tightly.*
- *Flip the bottles so that the bottle with the water is on top. Grasp the bottles around the necks and quickly swirl them in circles parallel to the floor.*
- *Set the bottles on a table, with the empty one on the bottom.*

Results The water swirls in a funnel shape as it pours from the top bottle. The falling water looks like a tornado.

Why? The funnel-shaped water moves through the small hole similar to the spiraling tail of a wind tornado. The water movement is due to the action of several forces, as is the movement of a tornado. Tornadoes in the United States form along fronts between cool, dry air from the west and warm, humid air from the Gulf of Mexico. The warm air quickly rushes upward, causing winds to rotate violently. Drops of water are formed as the water vapor condenses due to the low temperature and pressure inside the funnel. Tornadoes are visible because the large amount of liquid water in the cloud blocks the light as it does in a thunder-cloud. The debris picked up from the ground by the swirling winds adds to the color of the funnel cloud.

179

82. Micro-Bolt

Purpose To demonstrate that lightning produces radio waves.

Materials *radio with an antenna*
balloon, 9 in. (23 cm)
piece of fur or your own clean, dry, oil-free hair

Procedure

Note: Do this on a day with low humidity for best results.

■ *Turn the radio to a very low volume.*

■ *Inflate the balloon and tie it.*

■ *Quickly rub the balloon across a piece of fur about 10 times or rub the balloon against your clean, dry, oil-free hair.*

■ *Listen as you hold the balloon near, but not touching, the radio antenna.*

Results A single pop is heard from the radio as the balloon nears the antenna.

Why? The crackling sound of static during a thunderstorm is caused by radio waves, but not waves sent out from the radio station. The static sound is from radio waves sent out from lightning. Just as the built-up electrical charge on the balloon produced radio waves that were transmitted through the radio as a single popping sound, the electrical charges in lightning produce radio waves that are transmitted through the radio as the sounds we know as static. Radio waves are produced by electrical charges, and a flash of lightning produces 10,000 times the electric current needed for an electric iron.

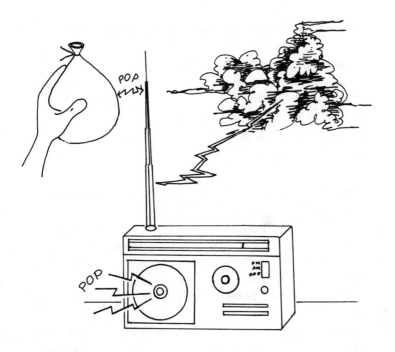

83. Bang!

Purpose To demonstrate the production of thunder.

Materials *paper lunch bag*

Procedure
- *Fill the bag by blowing into it.*
- *Twist the open end and hold it closed with your hand.*
- *Quickly and with force hit the bag with your free hand.*

Results The bag breaks and a loud noise is heard.

Why? Hitting the bag causes the air inside the bag to compress so quickly that the pressure breaks the bag. The air rushing out of the broken bag pushes the air outside the bag away from the bag. The air continues to move in a wave motion. A sound is heard when the moving air reaches an ear. Thunder is also a result of moving air. As lightning strikes, energy is given off that heats the air through which it passes. This heated air quickly expands, producing energetic waves of air called thunder.

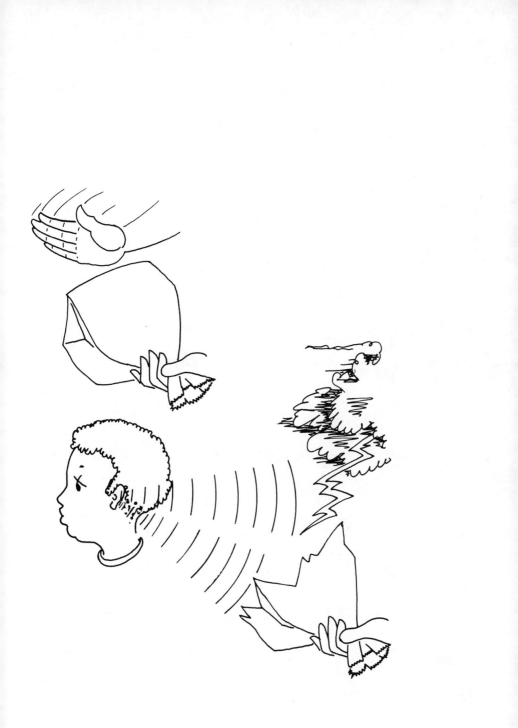

183

VII
Oceans

84. Wave Action

Purpose To demonstrate how wind produces water waves out at sea.

Materials *large, shallow pan*
drinking straw

Procedure
- *Fill the pan half full with water.*
- *Hold one end of the straw close to the surface of the water.*
- *Blow air across the water's surface.*
- *Blow gently, then harder.*

Results Waves formed on top of the water. The height of the waves varied with the change in strength of air flow.

Why? The energy of the moving air is transferred to the surface of the water, forming waves. The height of the waves depends on the speed of the wind. Moving air has energy, and this energy increases with the speed of the air. The energy from wind is given up as it hits the surface of the water. The energized water is pushed upward, forming a wave. As the energy passes through the water, ripples of waves move out from the end of the straw.

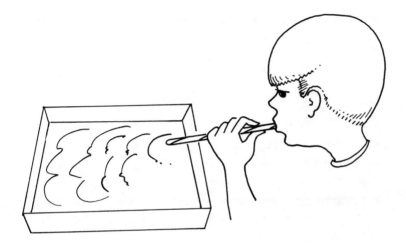

85. Waves

Purpose To demonstrate the motion of water waves.

Materials *Slinky® spring toy*
helper

Procedure
- *Lay the Slinky on the floor.*
- *Stretch the Slinky between you and your helper.*
- *Gently move one end of the Slinky back and forth several times.*
- *Change the speed of your back and forth movement by increasing and decreasing the distance the Slinky is moved.*

Results Up-and-down waves of motion move from one end of the Slinky to the other. The wave height increases with an increase in the distance that the end is moved.

Why? Waves that move up and down are called *transverse waves.* The high part of each wave is called the crest, and the lowest part is called the trough. The movement of the Slinky is a flat version of how water waves look and move from one point to another. Waves move from one end of the Slinky to the other, but the material in the Slinky stays in relatively the same place. Water molecules, like the rings in the Slinky, move up and down, but they do not move forward. Only the energy of each wave moves forward.

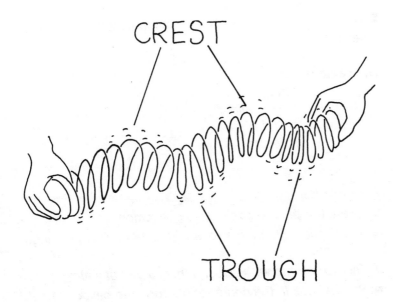

CREST

TROUGH

86. Bobber

Purpose To demonstrate the movement of water molecules in waves.

Materials *rock*
string
small balloon
bathtub
scissors
ruler

Procedure
- *Inflate the balloon to the size of a lemon.*
- *Attach the balloon to a rock with a 18 in. (45 cm) length of string.*
- *Fill the bathtub with about 6 in. (15 cm) of water.*
- *Set the rock in the center of the tub. The balloon should float on the surface with about 6 in. (15 cm) of extra string to allow it to move away from the rock.*
- *At the end of the tub, push your hand back and forth in the water for about 30 seconds to produce water waves.*
- *Observe the movement of the floating balloon.*

Results The balloon moves in a circle around the sunken rock.

Why? It appears that water waves move forward, but the actual water molecules are moving up and down in a circle. The movement of floating objects on a wave will be in a circle, with the diameter of the orbit equal to the height of the waves.

190

87. Bump!

Purpose To demonstrate the forward movement of wave energy.

Materials book
6 marbles

Procedure

- Lay the book on a flat surface such as a table or the floor.
- Open the book and place 5 of the marbles in the book's groove. Push the marbles tightly together and position the group in the center of the book.
- Place the free marble about 1 in. (3 cm) from the group of marbles, and thump it with your finger so that it moves forward and bumps into the end marble of the group.

Results The thumped marble stops when it strikes the end marble, and the marble on the opposite end of the group moves away from the group.

Why? The thumped marble has kinetic energy (energy of motion). Upon contact, this energy was transferred to the stationary marble, which transferred it to the marble next to it. Each marble transfers the energy to the next marble until the end marble receives it and moves forward. Any one of the marbles would have moved forward had it not been blocked by another marble. Water waves appear to move forward, but actually only the energy is transferred from one water molecule to the next, and each water molecule remains in relatively the same place. Like the end marble, the water near the beach moves forward, since there is nothing holding it back.

192

88. Currents

Purpose To determine if temperature affects the motion of water.

Materials *blue food coloring*
2 clear drinking glasses
2 coffee cups
jar, 1 quart (liter)
eyedropper
ice

Procedure

- *Fill the jar half full with ice, then add water to fill the jar. Allow to stand for 5 minutes.*
- *Fill one of the cups one-quarter full with the cold water from the jar.*
- *Add enough food coloring to the cold water to produce a dark blue liquid.*
- *Fill one of the glasses with hot water from the faucet.*
- *Fill the eyedropper with the cold colored water.*
- *Insert the tip of the eyedropper into the hot water in the glass and release several drops of colored water.*
- *Observe the movement of the colored water.*
- *Fill the second glass with cold water from the jar.*
- *Fill the remaining cup one-quarter full with hot water from the faucet and add enough food coloring to produce a dark blue liquid.*
- *Fill the eyedropper with the hot colored water.*
- *Insert the tip of the eyedropper in the cold water in the glass. Release several drops of the hot colored water.*
- *Observe the movement of the colored water.*

Results The hot colored water rose in the cold water, and the cold colored water sank in the hot water.

Why? Cold water contracts (gets closer together). Hot water expands (moves farther apart). This makes a drop of cold water more dense than a drop of hot water, because the molecules occupy less space. The denser cold water sinks and the less dense hot water rises. Convection currents are the results of water and air movement due to changes in temperature.

Cold colored water   Hot water

Hot colored water   Cold water

89. Sinker

Purpose To determine how density affects water movement.

Materials *glass bowl, 2 qt. (2 liter)*
table salt
measuring cup (250 ml)
measuring spoon, tablespoon (15 ml)
blue food coloring

Procedure

- *Fill the cup about three-quarters full (200 ml) with water.*
- *Add 6 tablespoons (90 ml) of salt to the water and stir.*
- *Pour in drops of food coloring to make the water a very deep blue color.*
- *Fill the bowl one-half full with water.*
- *Observe the bowl from the side as you slowly pour the blue, salty water down the side of the bowl.*

Results The colored water sinks to the bottom of the bowl, forming waves under the clear water above it.

Why? A density current is the movement of water due to the difference in the density of water. All sea water contains salt, but when two bodies of water mix, the water with the most salt will move under the lighter, less salty water.

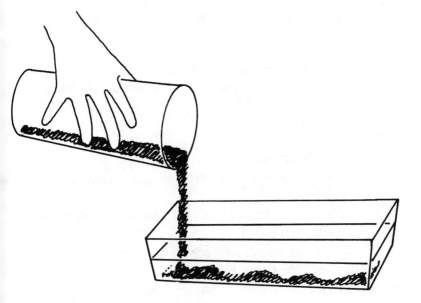

197

90. Movers

Purpose To demonstrate how winds cause surface currents.

Materials *shallow baking pan*
1 sheet of construction paper, any dark color
paper hole punch

Procedure

- *Fill the pan with water.*
- *Cut 10 circles from the construction paper with the hole punch.*
- *Place the paper circles on the surface of the water near the left side of the pan.*
- *Direct your exhaled breath across the surface of the water where the paper is floating.*
- *Observe the motion of the paper as you continue to blow.*

Results The paper circles move in a clockwise direction around the outside of the pan.

Why? Your breath starts a surface current (a horizontal movement of water). Surface currents on the earth begin in the tropics when powerful trade winds drive the ocean water before them. The water travels far away from where the wind starts the motion. The surface currents in the Northern Hemisphere move in a clockwise direction, and those in the Southern Hemisphere move counterclockwise. The rotation of the earth, changes in the temperature of the ocean water, and differences in the height of the ocean also contribute to the movement of surface currents.

198

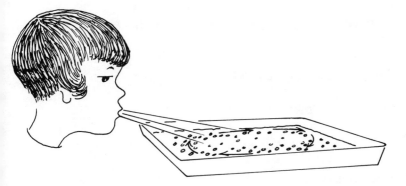

199

91. Twirler

Purpose To demonstrate the effect of the earth's rotation on wind and water currents.

Materials *construction paper*
scissors
pencil
ruler
eyedropper

Procedure

- *Cut an 8 in. (20 cm) diameter circle from the construction paper.*
- *Push the point of the pencil through the center of the circle.*
- *Place a drop of water on top of the paper near the pencil.*
- *Hold the pencil between the palms of your hands and twirl the pencil in a counterclockwise direction.*

Results The water drop swirls around the paper in a clockwise direction.

Why? The free-moving water is thrown forward, and the spinning paper moves out from under the water. Wind and water currents in the Northern Hemisphere are turned toward the right because of the rotation of the earth. Like the spinning paper, the moving earth moves out from under the unattached air and water, causing them to change direction. The deflection in the motion of objects due to the earth's rotation is called the *coriolis effect*.

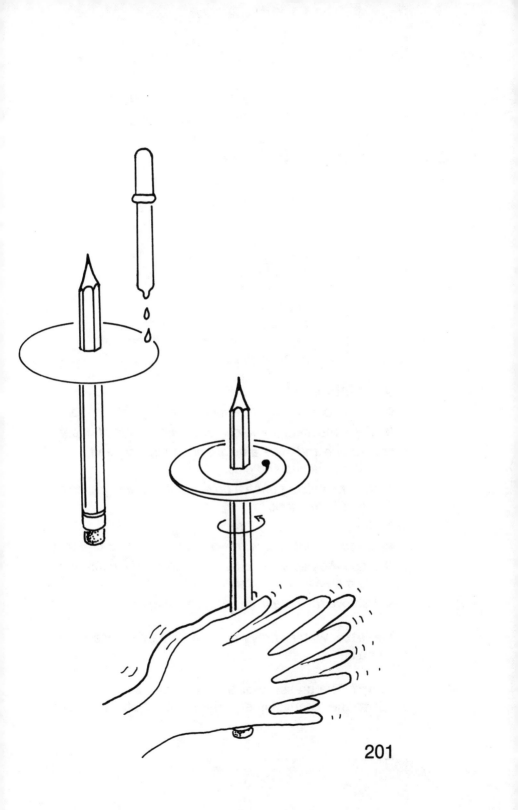

92. What's Up

Purpose To determine if water pressure is affected by volume.

Materials *large nail*
masking tape
marking pen
ruler
plastic jug, 1 gal. (4 liter)
paper cup, at least 4 in. (9 cm) tall
2 sheets of paper

Procedure

- *Place both sheets of paper on the edge of the table.*
- *Make one mark in the center of each sheet of paper.*
- *Measure and mark a height of 1 in. (2 cm) and 3 in. (7 cm) on the cup and plastic jug.*
- *Use the nail to punch a hole in the cup and jug on the 1 in. (2 cm) mark.*
- *Cover each hole with tape.*
- *Fill each container with water to the 3 in. (7 cm) mark.*
- *Place the papers side by side and set the containers on the marks in the center of each sheet.*
- *Remove the tape from each container.*

Results Water sprays out the same distance from each container.

Why? The pressure of the water is due to its depth and not to the total volume of the water. Water pressure at a depth of 2 yds. (2 m) is the same in a swimming pool as it would be in the ocean. The pressure of the water is due to the amount of water pushing down. Water pressure increases with depth, due to more water above.

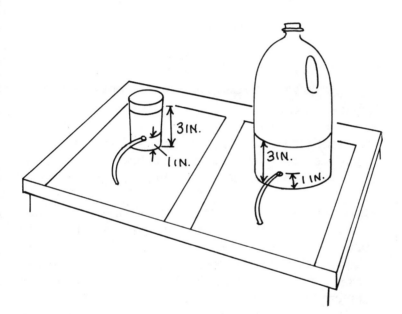

93. Divers

Purpose To determine how the buoyancy of ocean diving vessels changes.

Materials *drinking glass*
seltzer or club soda
raisins

Procedure
- *Fill the drinking glass three-quarters full with soda.*
- *Immediately add 5 raisins to the glass, one at a time.*
- *Wait and watch.*

Results Bubbles collect on the raisins. The raisins rise to the surface, spin over, and fall to the bottom of the glass, where more bubbles start to stick to them again.

Why? The raisins sink when their weight is greater than the upward buoyant force exerted by the liquid. The gas bubbles act like tiny balloons that make the raisins light enough to float to the surface. When the bubbles are knocked off at the surface, the raisins sink to the bottom until more bubbles stick to them. Submersibles are ocean research vessels that allow oceanographers to work deep beneath the ocean's surface. The vessels rise and sink in the water, as do the raisins, by changing their buoyancy. The ocean research vessels rise by releasing low-density liquids.

94. Weight Loss

Purpose To demonstrate how weight affects buoyancy.

Materials *plastic soft-drink bottle with lid, 2 qt. (2 liter)*
glass eyedropper

Procedure
- *Fill the plastic bottle with water to overflowing.*
- *Partially fill the eyedropper with water.*
- *Drop the eyedropper into the bottle of water. If the eyedropper sinks, remove it and squeeze some of the water out.*
- *Close the lid.*
- *Squeeze the sides of the bottle with your hands.*
- *Observe the level of the water inside the eyedropper.*

Results Squeezing causes the water to rise inside the eyedropper, and it sinks. When the bottle is released, the water level lowers inside the eyedropper, and the eyedropper floats to the surface.

Why? Squeezing the bottle increases the pressure inside, causing water to move into the open eyedropper. The extra water increases the weight of the eyedropper. It sinks because the upward push of the water is not great enough to hold up the now heavier eyedropper. The dropper rises when its weight is lessened by the loss of water. Submarines, like the dropper, move up and down in the water due to changes in weight. The submarine sinks by taking water into side tanks and rises by blowing that water out.

206

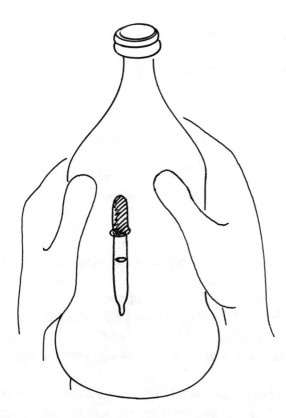

95. Salty Water

Purpose To determine how the ocean gets its salt.

Materials 2 paper cups
coffee filter
table salt
dirt
measuring spoon, tablespoon (15 ml)
pencil
1 sheet of black construction paper
modeling clay
plate

Procedure

■ Punch 6 holes in the bottom of the paper cup with the point of the pencil.

■ Place the coffee filter inside the cup.

■ In the empty cup, mix together 1 tablespoon (15 ml) of dirt and 1 tablespoon (15 ml) of salt.

■ Pour the dirt-salt mixture into the cup with the filter paper.

■ Place the sheet of black construction paper on the plate.

■ Use the clay to make short legs to support the cup above the black paper.

■ Pour 3 spoons of water on top of the dirt-salt mixture.

■ Allow the water to drain out of the cup and onto the black paper.

■ Allow the paper to dry. This process is speeded up if the paper is placed in the sun.

Results White crystals of salt form on the black paper.

208

Why? As the water flow through the soil, the salt dissolves in it and collects on the black paper. As the water evaporates from the paper, the dry salt is left behind. In nature, rainwater dissolves salt from the soil. If this water finds its way to rivers that flow into the ocean, the salt is added to the ocean water.

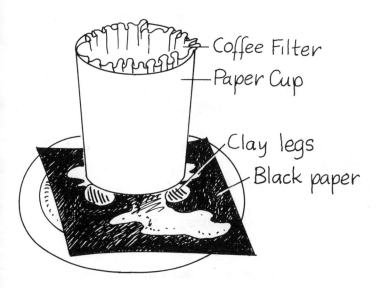

Coffee Filter
Paper Cup
Clay legs
Black paper

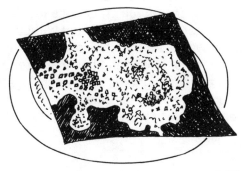

96. Hydrometer

Purpose To demonstrate how salt content is measured.

Materials *jar, 1 qt. (1 liter)*
modeling clay
table salt
measuring spoon, tablespoon (15 ml)
cap from a pen

Procedure

- *Fill the jar three-fourths full with water.*
- *Put enough clay in the pen's cap so that it sinks when placed in the jar of water.*
- *Add 1 tablespoon (15 ml) of salt to the water and stir.*
- *Observe any change in the position of the cap.*
- *Continue to add 1 tablespoon (15 ml) of salt at a time until 5 tablespoons (75 ml) have been added.*
- *Observe the position of the cap in the water after each tablespoon of salt has been added.*

Results The cap rises in the water as more salt is added.

Why? The upward push of the water on the cap is called the *buoyancy force*. This force increases with the weight of the water. Fresh water (water without salt) is less dense than salty water. As the salt content of the water increases, the water gets denser and has a greater buoyancy force, which lifts the cap higher in the water. The floating cap acts as a hydrometer, an instrument used to determine the salt content of water.

DAVIN'S
SALT

TABLESPOON

97. Solar Energy

Purpose To determine how solar energy affects ocean salinity (saltiness).

Materials *masking tape*
small bowl
plastic bag large enough to hold the bowl
table salt

Procedure

- *Cover the bottom of the bowl with a thin layer of salt.*
- *Fill the bowl one-half full with water and stir.*
- *Set the bowl inside the plastic bag and close the opening with tape.*
- *Place the bag in direct sunlight.*
- *After 24 hours, open the bag, touch the liquid collected on the plastic with your finger, and taste the liquid.*
  Note: Never taste anything in a laboratory setting unless you are sure that there are no harmful chemicals or materials. This experiment is safe, since only water and table salt are present.

Results The liquid inside the bag tastes like water.

Why? Light from the sun passes though the clear plastic and heats the surface of the salty water in the bowl as it does the surface of the ocean. The water evaporates, leaving the salt behind. The evaporated water in the bag condenses on the side of the plastic to form water drops of pure water, and the evaporated ocean water eventually falls as rain over the land. Salt in the soil is dissolved in the water as it moves across the land. The water finds its way back to the ocean via creeks, streams, and rivers, thus adding more salt to the salty sea water.

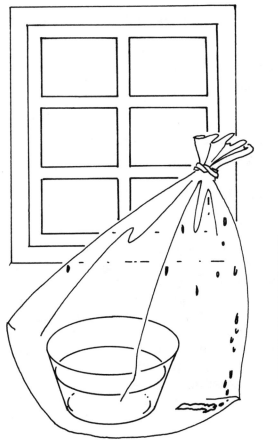

98. Floaters

Purpose To demonstrate how expanding ice saves water organisms.

Materials *bowl of water, 2 qt. (2 liter)*
1 ice cube

Procedure
- *Place a cube of ice in the bowl of water.*
- *Observe the position of the ice in the water.*

Results The ice floats on the surface of the water.

Why? Water begins to contract as it cools, like all substances. If it continued to contract, heavy blocks of ice would sink and stack in the bottom of bodies of water, killing water organisms. Water does not continue to contract, and unlike other materials, it starts to expand at 39.2° F (4° C), which makes it lighter than liquid water. Large ice masses float on the surface of water and even act as insulators to the water beneath. This special property of water is very significant. Life on this planet would cease to exist as we know it if water acted otherwise. Seas would freeze over, killing sea life, and the frozen seas would decrease the air temperature.

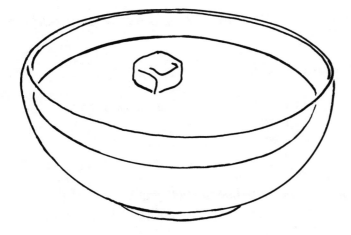

99. Super Cooled

Purpose To determine why the ocean is not frozen at the poles.

Materials *2 paper drinking cups*
table salt
measuring spoon, tablespoon (15 ml)
marking pen
freezer

Procedure

- *Fill both cups one-half full with water.*
- *Dissolve 1 tablespoon (15 ml) of salt into one of the cups of water.*
- *Mark an S on the cup containing the salt.*
- *Place both cups in the freezer.*
- *Observe the cup after 24 hours.*

Results The salty water does not freeze.

Why? Water freezes at 32°F (0° Celsius), but water with salt dissolved in it freezes at a lower temperature. The more dissolved salt, the lower the temperature required to freeze the solution. The dissolved salt blocks the water molecules from linking to form ice crystals. The salty water in the ocean can and does freeze when the temperature gets low enough. As the blocks of ice form at the poles, the salt is left in the water, making the water even saltier and harder to freeze, and thus liquid water exists in sub-zero temperatures.

216

100. Slosh!

Purpose To determine how the shape of shorelines affects the height of tides.

Materials *square baking pan*
round baking pan
pie pan
outdoor water source

Procedure

Note: This is an outdoor activity.

- *Fill each container to overflowing with water.*
- *Pick up one pan at a time and walk forward with the container held in front of you.*

Results The water spills more readily out of the square pan than out of the round baking pan or pie pan.

Why? Tides are the rise and fall of ocean waters and the entire ocean is affected from top to bottom. The difference in the rise and fall of the water is observed only along the shorelines. The pans represent shorelines of different shapes. The pie pan has a low, gently sloping side, and the square pan is more irregular than the round containers. Tides on low, gently sloping shores move in and out with little change. Exceptionally high tides occur along irregularly shaped shorelines. The Bay of Fundy in Nova Scotia rises as much as 42 ft. (13 m) during its high tide.

101. Tides

Purpose To determine the effect of centrifugal force on tides.

Materials *ruler*
scissors
paper drinking cup
string
measuring cup
pencil

Procedure

- *Use the point of a pencil to punch two holes across from each other beneath the top rim of the paper cup.*
- *Tie the ends of a 24 in. (60 cm) piece of string in these holes.*
- *Fill the cup one-half full with water.*
- *Hold the string and swing the cup around in a horizontal circle above your head several times.*

Note: You may want to do this experiment outside.

Results The cup turns sideways, but the water stays inside the spinning cup.

Why? The gravitational pull of the moon causes the ocean water to bulge on the side of the earth facing the moon. There is another bulge of water on the side of the earth opposite the moon. This second bulge results partly from the spinning of the earth. Spinning produces a centrifugal force that causes the revolving object to tend to fly away from the center around which it turns. The water in the cup moves outward because of centrifugal force, but the paper cup prevents it from flying away. The revolution of the earth around the sun produces a centrifugal force. The earth's rotation about its own axis contributes to this force. The result of this spinning is a bulging of the ocean waters on the earth, called high tides. The bulging water is prevented from spinning out into space by the earth's gravitational force.

Earth

Moon

Glossary

Abrasion: The erosion of a surface by grinding action such as moving sand.

Anemometer: Instrument used to measure wind speed.

Atmosphere: Layer of air above the earth.

Barometer: Instrument used to measure air pressure.

Caliche: (ka leé chee) Deposits of limestone (calcium carbonate) near or on the surface of the ground.

Center of Gravity: The point on an object where it can be balanced.

Centrifugal Force: A force that tends to move a rotating object away from the center of rotation.

Cloud: Mass of tiny raindrops in the sky.

Compression: Forces from opposite directions.

Condensation: The change of a gas to a liquid. Requires a loss of energy.

Contract: To move closer together.

Coriolis Effect: The deflection in the motion of objects due to the earth's rotation.

Current: A flow of moving water or air.

Dew: Moisture condensed from the air.

Dew Point: Temperature at which water vapor in the air condenses.

Dike: Vertical columns of magma intruded into bedrock (rock that forms the crust of the earth).

Dynamo Theory: The magnetic freed caused by the rotation of the earth.

Erosion: Wearing away.

Evaporation: The change of a liquid to a gas. Requires the gain of energy.

Expand: To move farther apart.

Fold: Bending of rock layers.

Fossil: Any impression or trace of organisms from past geologic times.

Frost: Feathery ice crystals formed when water vapor sublimes, changes from a gas directly to a solid.

Geyser: A funnel-shaped crack in the earth that periodically throws out jets of hot water and steam.

Glaciers: A large mass of ice that slowly moves.

Hydrometer: Instrument used to measure the density of a liquid.

Hydraulic Mining: Using powerful streams of water to mine metal.

Hydrosphere: Water on the surface of the earth.

Hygrometer: Instrument used to measure humidity.

Igneous Rock: Rock formed from magma (molten rock).

224

Isostasy: The equal up-and-down movement of the earth's crust.

Kinetic Energy: Energy of motion.

Laccolith: Dome-shaped hardened magma formed between rock layers.

Lava: Liquid rock that has reached the earth's surface.

Lightning: A flash of electricity through the atmosphere.

Limestone: A mineral composed of calcium carbonate.

Lithosphere: The solid part of the earth.

Magma: Liquid rock beneath the earth's surface.

Magnetic Field: Force field around a magnet produced by moving electrons.

Mantle: The middle layer of the earth located beneath the upper crust.

Metamorphic Rock: Rocks that have been changed by heat, pressure, chemical actions, or a combination of these.

Mid-Ocean Ridge: Mountain chain on the floor of the ocean from which magma rises and causes sea floor spreading.

Nephoscope: Instrument used to determine the direction of wind in the upper air.

Ore: A rock with enough metal content to make it profitable to extract.

Placer Ore: Metal particles that form a layer over rock.

Precession: A slow change or wobble in the direction of the earth's axis.

Psychrometer: Instrument used to measure humidity by comparing temperature between wet and dry bulb thermometers.

P-Wave: Fast seismic waves that move, like sound waves, as compression waves. These waves can travel through liquids and solids.

Radio Waves: Waves that are produced by electrical charges and travel at the speed of light.

Regelation: The refreezing of water produced by the melting of ice under pressure.

Revolve: To move around a central point, as the earth moves around the sun.

Rotate: To spin on one's own axis, as a wheel turns on an axes.

Sand Dune: A buildup of loose sand piled up by the wind.

Sedimentary Rock: Rock made of layers of sediments that have been cemented together.

Seismogram: Written record from a seismograph.

Sill: Thin sheets of hardened magma injected between sedimentary rock layers.

Solar Energy: Energy from the sun.

Static: Electrical disturbance in the air.

Sublime: When a gas changes directly to a solid or a solid changes directly to a gas. Examples: frost, dry ice, mothballs.

S-Waves: Seismic waves that move earth particles up and down as the wave energy moves forward. The wave can move only through solids.

226

Tension: A stretching or pulling force.

Thermometer: Instrument used to measure temperature.

Thunder: Loud noises caused by rapid compression of air as lightning passes through the atmosphere.

Tides: The rise and fall of the ocean due to gravitational attraction of the moon and sun plus the centrifugal force caused by the earth's rotation about the sun.

Topsoil: Upper soil surface. Rich in nutrients and minerals.

Transverse Wave: Waves that move material up and down as the energy of the wave moves forward.

Trench: Very deep ocean valleys.

Volcano: A mountain from which steam, ash, and lava are expelled through openings.

Wind: Movement of air.

Index

SCIENCE IS FOR EVERY KID!

WIN A FREE MAGNIFYING GLASS

We'd like to know about your favorite Janice VanCleave experiment.

Do you like to watch bacteria grow? Communicate with fireflies? Or are you happiest creating green blobs???????

Tell us about your most cherished science experiment . . . and don't waste a molecular minute!!!

The first 100 enthusiastic fans who respond will receive the official Janice VanCleave magnifying glass!

Just fill in the coupon below and mail to:

SCIENCE FOR EVERY KID **HEADQUARTERS / T. Moore**
John Wiley & Sons, 605 Third Avenue, New York, NY 10158

- -

SCIENCE FOR EVERY KID HEADQUARTERS

NAME _____ **AGE** _____

ADDRESS _____

_____

What's your favorite Janice VanCleave experiment? _____

_____

_____

Where did you buy this book? _____

What other books do you enjoy reading? _____

_____

Would you be interested in joining the Janice VanCleave *Science for Every Kid* **fan club?   YES** _____   **NO** _____

Membership in the *Science for Every Kid* **fan club entitles you to the official membership card, newsletters, and other surprises . . . and it's free!!!!!**